# LONGMAN
# COMMERCIAL
# COMMUNICATION

An intermediate course in English for
commercial correspondence and practice

## AJ Stanton and LR Wood

## Students' Book

**Longman Group UK Limited,**
*Longman House, Burnt Mill, Harlow,*
*Essex CM20 2JE, England*
*and Associated Companies throughout the world.*

First published 1988
Seventh impression 1992

Set in 10pt Baskerville

Printed in Hong Kong
WLEE/07

ISBN 0 582 85273 0

Cover photograph by 'The Stock Photobank – London'.

## ACKNOWLEDGEMENTS

We are grateful to the following for permission to reproduce copyright material:

The Author, R.B. Cannon for an adaptation of his article 'Four Profitable Ways...' from *The Guardian* 31.1.87; the Daily Telegraph plc for adapted articles 'Jobs for life' by Paul Nathanson, 'Learn Body Language' by Roland Gribben from *Daily Telegraph* 22.8.86, 11.9.86; Guardian Newspapers Ltd for adapted article 'Slow Payers owe £57bn and curb job Creation' by Clive Woodcok from *The Guardian* 19.11.86.

We are grateful to the following for permission to reproduce copyright illustrative material:

Bank of America for page 52; Barnabys Picture Library for page 52 (top and middle left); British Telecom International for page 89; Credit Lyonnais for page 52; Credit Suisse for page 52; The Financial Times for page 153; Handford Photography for page 102; Hongkong Bank for page 52; Lloyds Bank plc for pages 52 and 121 (left and right); Longman Photo Unit for page 73 (bottom left) and 146; Midland Bank plc for page 52; The Museum of London for pages 36 and 73 (top left); National Westminster Bank plc for page 52; Pictures Colour Library for page 52 (bottom right); The Stock Photobank – London for page 73 (top right); Tony Stone Photo Library/London for page 87; Zefa Picture Library (UK) Limited for page 135

# CONTENTS

# INTRODUCTION

This book is for intermediate students who wish to study English in a commercial context. The units teach the skills needed in this specialised area and provide practice in:

- business letters for job applications, enquiries, orders, replies to orders, packing instructions, making complaints and dealing with complaints, refusing orders
- memos, telex messages and informal notes
- oral summaries
- listening and note-taking
- reading and note-taking
- punctuation
- grammatical structures
- how to say numbers, weights and measures
- formal and informal style
- role-play in business situations
- business vocabulary
- project work
- describing diagrams

The book also contains information about:

- British commercial and financial institutions
- documents of international trade
- office technology
- insurance, transport, advertising
- types of business organisation

The book consists of nine main teaching units and three revision and consolidation units. There is a Teacher's Guide which contains answers, tapescripts and dictation passages. There is also a C90 cassette.

Students who are preparing for the London Chamber of Commerce and Industry's 'English for Business' examination and 'Spoken English for Industry and Commerce' examination and other business English examinations will find suitable practice material in this book.

# U N I T   O N E

**Exercise 1.1**   Read these questions and find the answers in the advertisement.

---

### Junior Accounts Clerk

required by well-established company to assist in a busy accounts office. Microcomputer and accounts experience essential. Good prospects for a young person willing to work hard.

**Salary circa £7,500**

For further details and an application form, please write to Mr T Donovan, Mercury Distribution Services Ltd, 110–112 Bethune Street, London E1A 6PK.

---

**a**   What kind of experience is required for this job?
**b**   Is there a chance of promotion?
**c**   Does the advertisement tell you the exact salary?
**d**   How can you get more information about this job?

**Exercise 1.2**   Read this letter from a private individual requesting an application form for a job.
Answer the questions that follow.

9 Station Road
Colchester
Essex
CO14YD — **Sender's address**

**Recipient's name and address** —
Mr T. Donovan
Mercury Distribution Services Ltd
110-112 Bethune Street
London
**Postcode** —
E1A 6Pk                              24th September 19 — — **Date**

**Salutation** — Dear Mr Donovan,

**Opening** —
Please send me details of, and an application form for, the post of Junior Accounts Clerk advertised in today's 'Standard.'

**Body** —
I have recently completed a one-year full-time course in Book-keeping and Office skills, which included practical experience with computers. Since leaving college, I have been working temporarily in a hotel and am now looking for a permanent position.

**Close** —
I hope that you will consider me for this post and I look forward to hearing from you.

**Ending** —
Yours sincerely

**Signature** —
Peter Mills

**Name** —
Peter Mills

*Check your understanding*   **a**   Why doesn't Peter Mills give full details about himself in this letter?
**b**   Why is he looking for a new job?
**c**   Does he seem to have the experience required for this job?

**Exercise 1.3**  Read these questions and find the answers in the advertisements on the opposite page.
Read the advertisements quickly. You do not need to understand every word. You need only find the information to answer the questions.

*Advertisement one*  **a**  Is the Oxford Street shop open now?
**b**  Do applicants require special qualifications?
**c**  How could you earn more than £7,500?
**d**  What do you think 'other benefits' means?

*Advertisement two*  **a**  What kind of insurance is this job concerned with?
**b**  Does the job require previous experience of insurance?
**c**  How do you apply for this job?

*Advertisement three*  **a**  What are the three skills needed for this job?
**b**  Is Mary Smith an employee of the shipping company?
**c**  What other fringe benefits can you name, apart from the ones mentioned here?

*Advertisement four*  **a**  Why does the bank need more staff?
**b**  What kind of experience is required?
**c**  How is the salary decided?

*Advertisement five*  **a**  What will the administrative assistant have to do?
**b**  What personal qualities are required?

**Exercise 1.4**  Write down the number of the advertisement that:

**a**  offers the highest salary
**b**  may offer the opportunity to work abroad
**c**  does not ask for previous experience
**d**  involves using the telephone a lot
**e**  involves contact with the public
**f**  asks for someone good with figures
**g**  offers training opportunities
**h**  asks for organising ability
**i**  requires experience of business machines
**j**  does not mention the name of the company where you will be working
(You may write more than one number.)

# Classified Advertisements APPOINTMENTS

**1**

**CHAPMANS CAMERAS LTD** require sales staff for their new Oxford Street branch opening soon. Applicants should have experience of working in a busy retail environment and a general interest in photography.

**SALARY £7,500 + COMMISSION + OTHER BENEFITS**
Ring Paul Barton on 01 742 6913 to arrange an interview.

**2**

## INSURANCE TRAINEE

£8,500 per annum plus bonus plus luncheon vouchers.

We are seeking a young ambitious person with mathematical ability, to be trained in all aspects of marine insurance. Full training will be given.

Call 01 600 9034 for further details and speak to Philip Robinson direct.

**Philip Robinson Insurance Brokers**

**3** ## PERSONAL ASSISTANT/SECRETARY

25–35 c £9,000 negotiable. Ref. HA/30

Our clients, a large shipping company, need a responsible, adaptable person with good typing and telex skills who can cope with figures.
Lots of telephone liaison.
Fringe benefits include luncheon vouchers, season ticket loan and private medical insurance.

Phone Mary Smith for further details on 01 700 9261.

**Pace Employment Consultants**

**4**

## BANKING OPPORTUNITIES

As a result of continuing expansion at our City branch, we are presently seeking the following staff:

**Experienced bank clerk**

This is an ideal opportunity for someone who has previous experience of banking, or a related field, and is able to cope with a wide variety of duties in a busy environment.

**Junior bank clerk**

This is an excellent training position for someone interested in a career in banking. You should have a good general education.

We work a 35-hour, 5-day week, and attractive salaries are offered for both positions, depending on age and experience.
If you have the right background and are interested in either of the above vacancies, write with full details to:

**Mr A Hutton, Manager, Finlays Bank plc**
32 Moor Street, London EC3

**5**

## Administrative Assistant Bi-lingual English/Italian

We organise conferences in Britain and abroad. We are looking for someone with the ability to work under pressure and to organise and communicate effectively. We need someone who pays attention to detail when liaising with committees and senior management.

Word-processing experience is essential, as is a good telephone manner. This is a position for a well-motivated person with initiative and a flexible attitude to a very varied job.

Salary scale £9,959 – £10,875 according to age and experience.

Please write with full details, or send your curriculum vitae, to:

**Mrs J Hobbs, Personnel Officer,**
**Robert Donaldson and Partners,**
**12 Manton Terrace, London W1**

*UNIT ONE*

**Exercise 1.5**
*Vocabulary*

Find a word or phrase in the advertisement which means:

**a**  selling to the public                                                    1
**b**  payment according to how much you sell                  1
**c**  an additional payment for good work                        2
**d**  things your employer gives you in addition to
       your salary                                                          3
**e**  a similar type of work                                            4
**f**  absolutely vital                                                      5
**g**  able to move easily between the different tasks
       required in your job                                               5
**h**  keen to be successful                                            2
**i**  ability to work without supervision                         5
**j**  looking for                                                           4
**k**  open to discussion                                                3

(The number tells you in which advertisement to look.)

**Exercise 1.6**
*Abbreviations*

This advertisement uses a lot of abbreviations. Find out what these abbreviations stand for by looking at the other advertisements.
Write this advertisement out in full.

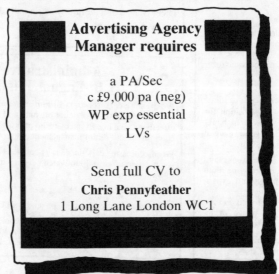

**Advertising Agency
Manager requires**

a PA/Sec
c £9,000 pa (neg)
WP exp essential
LVs

Send full CV to
**Chris Pennyfeather**
1 Long Lane London WC1

**Exercise 1.7**
*Listen to this*

Listen to the telephone conversation between Graham Forbes and Paul Barton, the Personnel Manager of Chapmans Cameras. Paul Barton is trying to find out if it is worth inviting Graham for an interview.
In order to have a record of the phone call, Paul Barton has a checklist which he fills in as he talks to Graham. Complete this checklist.

```
TELEPHONE ENQUIRIES - JOB APPLICATIONS


NAME:

ADDRESS:

PRESENT EMPLOYER:

POSITION IN FIRM:

PRESENT SALARY:

WORK EXPERIENCE:

REASON FOR LEAVING PRESENT JOB:

APPLICANT'S MANNER:

                        Polite          □
                        Rude            □
                        Articulate      □
                        Inarticulate    □
                        Interested      □
                        Bored           □
                        Confident       □
                        Nervous         □



    ACTION TAKEN:

                        Rejected            □
                        Interview arranged  □
                        Asked to call back  □
                        Application form sent □
```

**Exercise 1.8**
*Say what you have heard*

Paul Barton was impressed with Graham and considers him a strong candidate for the job. He talks to a colleague about him.

Work with a partner.

Say what you know about GRAHAM. Use your completed checklist to help you make questions and answers.

| | |
|---|---|
| PAUL BARTON: | This man Forbes seems to be the sort of person we are looking for. |
| COLLEAGUE: | Does he have experience of selling? |
| PAUL BARTON: | Oh yes, he . . . |

9

**Exercise 1.9**
*Letters of application*

**a** What information would you include in a letter of application for a job? Work with a partner and make a list.

**b** Now read Sally Brooke's letter of application for the job of Bi-lingual Administrative Assistant (see advertisement on page 7). Has Sally included all the points on your list?

```
Kolleg 16/12
1030 Vienna
Austria


Mrs J Hobbs
Personnel Officer
Robert Donaldson and Partners
12 Manton Terrace
LONDON   W1                                        25 January 19-


Dear Mrs Hobbs,

Bi-lingual Administrative Assistant

I have seen your advertisement for a Bi-lingual Administrative Assistant, in
last Friday's 'Guardian', and wish to apply for this post.

I am twenty-six years old and have a Bi-lingual Secretary's Diploma.   At
present I am working for a publishing company in Vienna, but for personal
reasons I would like to return to the United Kingdom.

When I was at school I specialised in languages and passed advanced
examinations in French, German and Italian.   On leaving school, I went to
Hammersmith Secretarial College, where I obtained my Diploma.   After
finishing my course, I spent a year in Italy, where I worked as a hotel
receptionist and continued to study Italian.

After I had returned to England, I went to London and started working for
'The London Informer', selling classified advertising by telephone.   While
I was working for this newspaper, I took an advanced course in 'Micro-Computing
for the Office' in the evenings.   After one year in this job I started work
for IPCO, the international publishing company, in Vienna.   In this job I
have to assist in the organisation of meetings.   My work involves liaison with
senior management in various departments.

Mr Joseph Keller, the Senior Manager of IPCO International, Vienna has
agreed to give you any further information you require about my work.
Mr Ian Jackson, the Advertising Manager of 'The London Informer',
5 Broad Court, London EC3, has also agreed to act as a referee.

I will be in London from 3rd March to 1st April and will be available for
interview during those four weeks.

I look forward to hearing from you.

Yours sincerely,

S. Brooke

Sally Brooke (Miss)
```

# UNIT ONE

**Exercise 1.10**
*Check your understanding*

a  How did Sally learn about this job?
b  Why does she want to leave her present job?
c  What was her first job?
d  Why is she only available for interview from 3rd March to 1st April?

**Exercise 1.11**
*Vocabulary*

Find a word or phrase in Sally's letter which means:

a  a job
b  to help
c  newspaper advertisements grouped by subject
d  someone you ask to give information about you to a possible employer

**Exercise 1.12**
*Making a checklist*

The advertisement asks for 'a good telephone manner'. Sally says that she has had a job 'selling classified advertising by telephone'.

Work with a partner.
Study the advertisement and make a checklist of what is required for the job. Match Sally's experience and qualifications with your checklist. You should have two headings – REQUIREMENTS OF JOB and WHAT SALLY SAYS IN HER LETTER.

**Exercise 1.13**
*Choosing applicants*

Caroline Campbell applied for the same job as Sally Brooke. She didn't send a full letter of application. She sent her Curriculum Vitae and a short covering letter.

Work in groups of three or four.
a  Compare Caroline's letter and Curriculum Vitae with the advertisement. Match her qualifications and experience with the requirements of the job. Make a checklist like the one you made for Exercise 1.12.

**b** Which applicant, Sally or Caroline, would you choose, and why?

Use these expressions to say what you think.

*Expressing opinions:*

| | | |
|---|---|---|
| I think that | | should get the job because . . . |
| In my opinion | Caroline Campbell | is the better |
| | Sally Brooke | candidate . . . |
| It seems to me that | | is the right person . . . |

*Agreeing:*
I agree with you, but . . .
That's true, but what about . . .
I think you're right about that, but on the other hand . . .

*Disagreeing:*
I don't agree with you . . .
I'm afraid I disagree with you . . .          because . . .
I think you might be wrong about that . . .

65 Earlsfield Road
Epsom
Surrey
EL3 2BK

Mrs J Hobbs
Personnel Officer
Robert Donaldson and Partners
12 Manton Terrace
London W1                              21st January 19 —

Dear Mrs Hobbs,

  I wish to apply for the position of Bi-lingual Secretary, which was advertised in today's 'Guardian'.

  I enclose my Curriculum Vitae. Please let me know if there is any further information you require.

  Yours sincerely
  Caroline Campbell

  Caroline Campbell (Mrs)

Enc. Curriculum Vitae

| | |
|---|---|
| Name: | CAROLINE CAMPBELL |
| Address: | 32 Earlsfield Road, Epsom, Surrey |
| Telephone: | Home: Epsom (03727) 59643<br>Work: Epsom (03727) 54343 ext 31 |

Personal Details:

| | |
|---|---|
| Date and Place of Birth: | 3rd May 1963, Chiswick, London |
| Marital Status: | Married, no children |
| Availability for Employment: | Present employer requires one month's notice |
| Mobility: | I am able to travel, but would prefer not to be away from home longer than four weeks |

Qualifications:

| | |
|---|---|
| Professional: | Diploma in Secretarial Skills (Distinction) |
| Languages: | Fluent French and Italian |
| Education: | Primrose Lane Comprehensive School, Chiswick, London W4<br>1974-1980<br>Advanced examination passes in English and Italian<br><br>Epsom College<br>1986-1987<br>Diploma in Secretarial Skills |

Career Details:

| | |
|---|---|
| September 1980 | Clerk, British Air |
| February 1981 | Stewardess, British Air<br>'Stewardess of the Year' 1984 |
| March 1985 | Senior Stewardess |
| July 1986 | Left British Air |
| August 1987 | Secretary to the Assistant Manager, McCann, Knott and Crocker Advertising Agency |
| April 1989 | Secretary/Personal Assistant to the Senior Sales Manager, Speedtel Ltd. |

Referees:

Mrs J Browning
Senior Sales Manager
Speedtel Ltd
70 Bush Lane
Epsom
Surrey    EL3 4TW

Mr M Parker
Assistant Manager
McCann, Knott and Crocker
2 Monmouth Row
London WC2 1AR

**Exercise 1.14**   Complete the following letter. There are 25 words missing. Refer to the other letters in the unit for help.

95 Hertford Road
London W5 1EL

Mr A Hutton
Manager
Finlays Bank plc
32 Moor Street
London EC3                                                    23rd January 19—

Dear Mr Hutton,

                    Experienced Bank Clerk

    I _____ (1) just _____ (2) your advertisement _____ (3) an experienced Bank Clerk _____ (4) today's 'Guardian' and _____ (5) to apply for this _____ (6).

    I am twenty years _____ (7) and since leaving school I have been working _____ (8) a clerk/cashier _____ (9) a small Building Society.

    At school I _____ (10) examinations in English, Maths, Economics, Geography and Biology. _____ (11) I do not have experience _____ (12) banking, my present job _____ (13) dealing with the public and handling large amounts _____ (14) cash. I frequently have _____ (15) use computers, and I am currently _____ (16) evening classes _____ (17) computer programming. I enjoy what I do now, but I would like _____ (18) work _____ (19) a larger company _____ (20) I want to gain experience of a wider _____ (21) of duties and to further my career.

    Mr A Pullen, the Manager of the Acton Branch of the Greenslade Building Society, 3 High Street, Acton, has _____ (22) to act as one of my _____ (23) and you _____ (24) also contact Mr R Miller, Headmaster, Middleton Comprehensive School, Green Lane, Chiswick, London W4.

    I look forward to _____ (25) from you.

                    Yours sincerely,
                    Alice Taylor
                    Alice Taylor (Miss).

**Exercise 1.15**
*Preparing a letter*

Is John Norris a suitable applicant for the National Motorparts job?

Work with a partner.
Compare John's notes for his letter of application with the advertisement. Match his qualifications, training and experience with the requirements of the job. Would you include in his letter all the information John has noted?

THE CHURCHMINSTER TIMES 7 July 19–

## NATIONAL MOTORPARTS LTD

are looking for a regional manager (South-West) for their nationwide chain of stores catering for motorists. We require an energetic, self-motivated individual with experience of supervising staff and dealing with the public.
Age range 25–35.
We offer a starting salary of £12,000 plus bonus, a prestige car and other fringe benefits.
Applicants need not have experience of the motor trade, although this would be an advantage, but they should be knowledgeable and enthusiastic about cars. Full training will be given.

Write with full details, or send C.V., giving the names of two referees, to:
**Mr R Jenkins, NMP Ltd,**
2 High Street, Churchminster, Dorset CH1 2MP

Here are the notes John Norris made to prepare his letter.

| | |
|---|---|
| July 1982 | left school |
| Sept 1982 | went to Wessex College to study Commerce |
| | obtained Higher National Diploma |
| July 1984 | trainee manager at Star Supermarket, Churchminster; took evening course in book-keeping |
| Jan 1987 | deputy manager BFI Furniture Ltd, Fallowfield |
| Sept 1988 | manager, Star Supermarket, Churchminster |

Other qualifications and skills:

Completed first-aid course
passed Advanced Motorists Test – first time!
hobbies : rally-driving and tennis

referees: J Pearson, Head of Department of Business Studies, Wessex College, Churchminster Dorset
W Pinfold, Chairman, Star Group plc, 1 Tower Street, London SE1 5TE

**Exercise 1.16**
*Letter writing*

Write a complete letter of application for John Norris, correctly laid-out.

*Useful expressions*

When you apply for a job, you may want to give information about yourself in chronological order. Here are some phrases you can use for this purpose.

*On leaving school, I went to . . .*
*On returning to England, I obtained . . .*
*Having gained a certificate in . . .*
*Having obtained my diploma in . . .*
*After I had finished college, I started . . .*
*Since leaving college, I have been . . .*
*Since leaving school, I have worked as a . . .*
*After I had worked for the company for a year, I became . . .*
*While I was living in Italy, I studied . . .*
*While I was working there, I took a course in . . .*
*During the two years I worked for this company, I organised . . .*
*During my employment with this company, I continued to study . . .*

**Exercise 1.17**
*Focus on punctuation:*
*CAPITAL LETTERS*

Study the way in which CAPITAL LETTERS are used in the following sentences.

**a**  Mr Simon Crocker is the Managing Director of the McCann, Knott and Crocker Advertising Agency.
**b**  I could come for an interview on Wednesday, 26th June.
**c**  She studied French and Italian at the University of Manchester.
**d**  The company placed an advertisement in 'The Times'.

Re-write these sentences using CAPITAL LETTERS where appropriate.

**e**  write to mrs j baxter, personnel officer, robert downing and partners, 40 church street, london sw25.
**f**  he is unable to come on friday, 10th september.
**g**  she studied german at heidelberg university.
**h**  i sold classified advertising space for 'the guardian' from march 1986 to may 1987.

**Exercise 1.18**
*How to say it:*
*Names, addresses and*
*telephone numbers*

It is often necessary to dictate a name and address over the telephone.
Study the example to find out how to do it.

## UNIT ONE

Janet Robinson
30 Brookside Road
London W13 2PT
Tel: 544 0043

My name is Janet Robinson. That's J.A.N.E.T. That's my first name. R.O.B.I.N.S.O.N. That's my surname. My address is thirty – 3.0. – Brookside Road. That's B.R. double O.K. S.I.D.E. Road, London. And the postcode is W thirteen – one three – 2PT – P for Peter, T for Tom. And my phone number is 01 – that's the code for London, 5 double 4 double 0 43. Could you read it back to me, please

Work with a partner.
Student A dictates these names, addresses and telephone numbers. Student B must write them down. (See next page.)

Mrs Audrey Carrington
50 Poachers Walk
Brighton
Sussex
BR2 7LM
Tel. 0273 6881

**Air Mail**

Julio Perez
Avda San Martin 1201
Buenos Aires
Argentina

Pierre Chevalier
21 rue des Eaux Claires
38000 Grenoble
France

**NOTES**

Philip Thompson
15 Avoncroft Way
Flitton
Gloucestershire
GL6 8BT

Tel: 0452 2244

**Air Mail**

Ingrid Bergvill
Hedgehaugsveien 19
Stavanger
Norway

**ADDRESS BOOK**

CHAN KAM HING
2/F, 90 Nathan Road
Kowloon
Hong Kong

Tel: 3-7131605

Sir Hamish MacGregor
Atholl House
By Blair Atholl
Morayshire
Scotland

# UNIT ONE

As you listen to your partner and write down the names
and addresses, you might want to say:

| | |
|---|---|
| *How do you spell it?* | *Is that one word?* |
| *Could you spell it for me, please?* | *Is that on the same line?* |
| *Could you repeat it, please?* | *What's after the 'm'?* |
| *Is that your surname?* | *Does it begin with a capital letter?* |
| *Sorry?* | *Is that a 't' or a 'd'?* |

 **Exercise 1.19**
*Listen to this*

Mary Smith of Pace Employment Consultants has left her
office for a short time. She has left the telephone answering
machine switched on. Several people phone to enquire about
various jobs. When Mary returns she listens to the messages
and transfers the information onto a special form.
Copy this form into your notebook. Listen to the messages on
the cassette and complete your form.

| NAME | ADDRESS | TELEPHONE | REFERENCE |
|---|---|---|---|
| Jane Parkinson | 74A Uppingham Mansions, London NW1 | 260 1299 | HA/30 |

**Exercise 1.20**
*Letter writing*

Jennifer Stephens applied for a job with a shipping company.
She received, completed and sent off an application form.
Can you re-arrange these words and phrases to form the
reply that she received? You will then have a correctly laid-
out letter.

BR1 8AT
Miss Jennifer Stephens
Bristol
61 Clifden Avenue

**SURESPEED SHIPPING plc**
5 WATER LANE, LONDON EC1 2PY
TEL: 01-662 5587   TELEX: 566789

Dear Miss Stephens

    We look forward

          30 January 19-

       Charles Jackson

Thank you for               (see enclosed leaflet)

          Managing Director

   at 9.30 a.m.

         and we would like you

Yours sincerely,

     We will refund        for an interview

   take place

       your completed application form

   to attend

         to seeing you a week on Monday

      Your qualifications

interest us               your travelling expenses

at our office at the above address    Enc  travel expenses claim form and map

   and experience

   The interview will        on Monday 10 February

**Exercise 1.21**
*Letter writing*

When Jennifer Stephens consulted the railway timetable in order to plan her journey from Bristol to London, she found the following information.

Swansea – Cardiff – Newport – London

| Cardiff | | Bristol Parkway | | Paddington |
|---|---|---|---|---|
| Swansea | Newport | 6 miles north of city centre | Reading | |

So — Saturday only

| Mondays to Saturdays | So | | | | | | | | | | |
|---|---|---|---|---|---|---|---|---|---|---|---|
| Swansea | —— | —— | 0550 | —— | 0630 | 0700 | 0730 | 0835 | 0935 | 1035 |
| Neath | —— | —— | 0601 | —— | 0641 | 0711 | 0741 | 0846 | 0946 | 1046 |
| Port Talbot Parkway | —— | —— | 0608 | —— | 0649 | 0718 | 0748 | 0854 | 0954 | 1054 |
| Bridgend | —— | —— | 0620 | —— | 0701 | 0730 | 0800 | 0906 | 1006 | 1106 |
| Cardiff Central | 0600 | 0620 | 0645 | —— | 0725 | 0755 | 0825 | 0930 | 1030 | 1130 |
| Newport | 0614 | 0634 | 0700 | —— | 0740 | 0810 | 0840 | 0945 | 1045 | 1145 |
| Bristol Parkway | 0635 | 0654 | 0735 | 0756 | 0805 | 0835 | 0900 | 1005 | 1105 | 1205 |
| Swindon | 0704 | 0723 | 0749 | —— | 0831 | 0900 | —— | 1036 | 1135 | 1235 |
| Reading (arrive) | 0734 | 0749 | 0815 | —— | —— | —— | 0949 | 1101 | 1201 | 1301 |
| Slough (arrive) | 0818 | —— | —— | —— | —— | —— | —— | 1150 | 1250 | 1350 |
| London Paddington | 0835 | —— | 0935 | 0940 | 1020 | 1050 | 1110 | 1130 | 1230 | 1330 |

| Sundays | | | | | | | | | | |
|---|---|---|---|---|---|---|---|---|---|---|
| Swansea | —— | 0550 | 0630 | 0700 | 0730 | 0825 | 0855 | 0935 | 1035 | —— |
| Neath | —— | 0601 | 0641 | 0711 | 0741 | 0836 | 0907 | 0946 | 1046 | —— |
| Port Talbot Parkway | —— | 0608 | 0649 | 0718 | 0748 | 0843 | 0915 | 0954 | 1054 | —— |
| Bridgend | —— | 0620 | 0701 | 0730 | 0800 | 0855 | 0930 | 1006 | 1106 | —— |
| Cardiff Central | 0600 | 0645 | 0725 | 0755 | 0825 | 0920 | 0956 | 1030 | 1130 | —— |
| Newport | 0614 | 0700 | 0740 | 0810 | 0840 | 0935 | 1011 | 1045 | 1145 | —— |

**a** What is Jennifer's problem?

**b** Write a correctly laid-out letter to Surespeed.

Refer to letter ........... *Thank you for your letter*

Refer to timetable ..... *I have consulted . . . and discovered . . .*

Explain problem ....... *Unfortunately, this means . . .*

Suggest solution........ *I wonder if it would be possible to . . .*

Close ....................... *Please let me know if . . .*

## The City of London

One of the most dramatic events in the history of the City of London was the Great Fire in 1666. It burned for six days and was described by Samuel Pepys, the famous diarist, who witnessed it, as 'a most horrid, malicious, bloody flame'. It destroyed almost all of the City, with the result that today there are hardly any really old buildings in this area – only a few stretches of Roman city wall and the Tower of London, which is just outside the City boundary. After the fire, the famous architect, Sir Christopher Wren, built St Paul's Cathedral to replace St Paul's Church,which had been destroyed in the fire. He also built many other churches in the city and a tall column, known as The Monument, to mark the spot where the fire started, in a baker's shop in Pudding Lane.

# UNIT ONE

Although there are few old buildings, there are plenty of traditional customs and ceremonies celebrated in the City. Every November the Lord Mayor's Show takes place, in which the new Lord Mayor of London proceeds, in a horse-drawn coach, through the streets of the city, from his official residence, Mansion House, to the Royal Courts of Justice. This is a well known tourist attraction. It dates from medieval times when the Lord Mayor wished to give an impressive display of his wealth and power. Another aspect of medieval London which has lasted into modern times is the Guild or Livery Company. Centuries ago, tradesmen such as bakers, goldsmiths and fishmongers formed themselves into societies, or guilds, which regulated the way they carried out their trade by controlling weight, quality and price. Today, these guilds still exist, but their members have little or no connection with the original trade and engage in social activities and perform charitable and educational functions. Several schools and hospitals are supported by guilds.

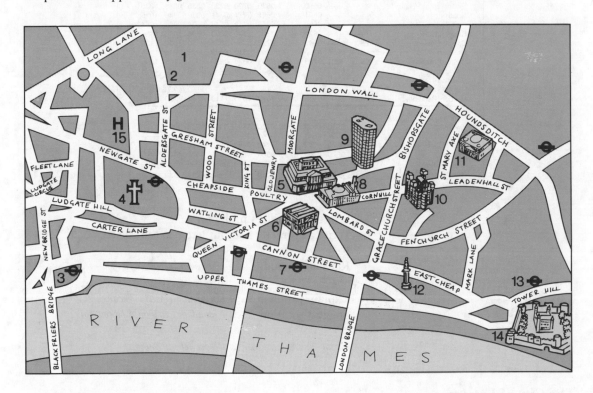

KEY

1 Barbican

2 Museum of London

3 Blackfriars Station

4 St Pauls Cathedral

5 Bank of England

6 Mansion House

7 Cannon Street Station

8 Royal Exchange

9 Stock Exchange

10 Lloyd's of London

11 Baltic Exchange

12 Monument

13 Tower Hill Station

14 Tower of London

15 St Bartholomew's Hospital

# UNIT ONE

The City of London covers quite a small area and in a short walk, many interesting buildings can be seen. There is Smithfield, the wholesale meat market – an unusual sight in this centre for financial services. There is the Old Bailey, the Central Criminal Court, where the most important criminal trials take place. Visible from most parts of the City is the National Westminster Tower, the tallest building in the whole of London. Almost as high are the three towers of the Barbican, an area of residential accommodation, in a place where over half a million people work, but only about 5,000 live. One of the most striking buildings in the City is the new Lloyd's building, opened in 1986, which is thought by many people to resemble an oil refinery. The demolition of old buildings often enables archeologists to do some 'rescue archeology' on the site before the new building is constructed. The things they find are displayed in the Museum of London, just in front of the Barbican, where the history of London is presented from pre-historic times to the present day.

**Exercise 1.22**
*Giving directions*

Work with a partner.
Study the map of the City of London on page 20.
Read the following directions to your partner, who should then tell you where he or she has arrived.

Turn right outside Tower Hill Underground station. Walk down Tower Hill keeping to the right and take the first right into Mark Lane. Go straight on. Then turn left into Fenchurch Street. Go straight on, cross Gracechurch Street into Lombard Street. Go over the crossroads into Poultry and take the third street on your right. Then turn left into Gresham street. Take the first left, immediately turn right and go straight ahead. Where are you?

Give directions to go on foot from:

a   Cannon Street Station to the Museum of London
b   Blackfriars Station to the Bank of England
c   the Baltic Exchange to Ludgate Circus
d   the Barbican to London Bridge

**Exercise 1.23**
*Things to find out*

Find out about one of these topics and report what you have learnt either in writing or as a short talk.

a   Samuel Pepys and his diary
b   The Great Fire of London
c   Markets in London
d   Guilds, or similar organisations of tradesmen in your own country.

# UNIT TWO

## YOU'RE ALWAYS IN WITH AUTOCOMM

For as little as **£4.99 per week plus a deposit of £575**, you can have a phone in your car which keeps you in constant touch with your customers, clients or office. Anywhere in the world. The **Autocomm** is a fully-portable telephone. Use it in a taxi, use it at home, use it anywhere you like. For instant worldwide communication. A 30-minute video film which shows how the **Autocomm system** can improve your business efficiency is available.

For more information about the phones in our range contact

**Speedtel plc, 70 Bush Lane, Epsom, Surrey EL3 4TW. Tel: 0372 4343**

**Exercise 2.1**
*Points for discussion*

a  How does this phone help business people?
b  Can you think of any disadvantages of this phone?
c  Which words tell you that you may have to pay more than £4.99 per week for an Autocomm phone?
d  Where would you find full information about the Autocomm system?

**Exercise 2.2**  Study this letter of enquiry, which Speedtel received in response to their advertisement.

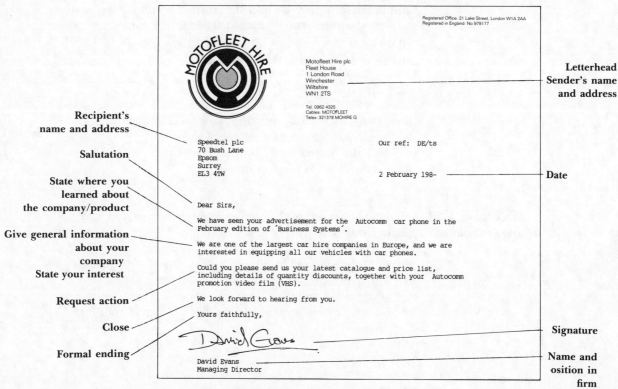

## UNIT TWO

*Check your understanding*

**A**

**a** Why is Motofleet interested in portable phones?

**b** Why might Motofleet get a discount?

**c** Why does the letter begin 'Dear Sirs'?

**d** How is the ending different from the endings of the letters in Unit One?

**B**

Now read the letter again.

Then close your book and, working with a partner, give an ORAL SUMMARY of the letter. Your partner should keep the book open and remind you of anything you forget. Here are some expressions that you can use:

*The letter is from . . . and it's addressed to . . .*
*It's about . . .*
*Mr Evans begins/ends by saying that. . .*
*He goes on to say that . . .*
*He asks if . . .*
*The letter is signed 'David Evans' . . .*

And here are some expressions your partner might use:

*You forgot to mention . . .*
*What about . . . ?*
*You missed out the bit about the . . .*

*Focus on functions:*
*What should you say in a*
*letter of enquiry?*

**1** Say where you saw the advertisement.

**2** Give some general information about your business.

**3** State your general reason for writing.

**4** Request action.

**5** Close the letter.

**6** Add a formal ending.

(Yours faithfully – if the salutation is Dear Sirs)

(Yours sincerely – if the salutation is Dear Mr/Mrs/Miss/Ms)

**A** Match the sentences in David Evans's letter with the functions listed above.

E.g. 1 Say where you saw the advertisement
'We have seen your advertisement for the Autocomm car phone in the February edition of "Business Systems".'

**B** Match the sentences below with the list of functions.

E.g. 5 Close the letter.
f We look forward to receiving your reply.

## UNIT TWO

Some functions can be matched with more than one sentence.

**a**  Please send us your latest catalogue and price list.

**b**  We are one of the largest importers of . . .

**c**  We have seen your advertisement in today's 'Guardian'.

**d**  We are interested in importing your range of . . .

**e**  Could you please send us some samples of . . .

**f**  We look forward to receiving your reply . . .

**g**  We have read your advertisement in this month's edition of . . .

**h**  We are a company which specialises in/imports . . .

**i**  We would appreciate it if you would send us more information about . . .

**j**  We have seen your advertisement in 'The Times' of 22nd January.

**k**  We are interested in purchasing . . .

**C**

Work with a partner. Student A should say what the functions of a letter of enquiry are.

  Use these words:

Firstly, Secondly, Thirdly, Next, Then, Finally
E.g. 'Firstly, you should say where you saw the advertisement . . .'
Student B should check what A says by looking at the list of functions.

**Exercise 2.3**  Mr King, of Across Africa Safaris Ltd, has seen this advertisement in 'Adventure' magazine and is writing for a catalogue and price list.

SHIPTONS OFFER THE LARGEST SELECTION OF RANGER VEHICLES IN THE COUNTRY.
FULLY GUARANTEED
UK AND EXPORT DEALERS
NEW AND USED MODELS
VEHICLES CAN BE MODIFIED
TO CUSTOMERS' REQUIREMENTS.
RUGGED AND RELIABLE –
RANGERS GO ANYWHERE IN THE
ROUGHEST CONDITIONS

**SHIPTONS**
SHIPTONS CROSS COUNTRY VEHICLES LTD
359 MOTTINGHAM ROAD   GREENWICH
LONDON SE10 2AF   UNITED KINGDOM
Tel: 01 305 7878   Telex: 342235

## UNIT TWO

Complete the letter.
Refer to the list of functions on pages 23–24 to help you.

---

Independence Way
Nairobi
Kenya

**Across Africa Safaris Ltd**

Tel: Nairobi 422305
Cables: TRANSAFRICAN
Telex: 896542

Shiptons Cross Country Vehicles Ltd
359 Mottingham Road
Greenwich
London SE10 2AF
United Kingdom

2 April 19–

Dear Sirs,

We have _____ (1) your advertisement _____(2) Ranger Vehicles _____ (3) the March _____ (4) of 'Adventure' magazine.

We are a company _____ (5) specialises _____ (6) overland safaris for tourists and, _____ (7) our business is expanding rapidly, we are _____ (8) in _____ (9) some new vehicles.

We would therefore _____ (10) it if you _____ (11) send us your _____ (12) catalogues and price lists.

We look forward to _____ (13) from you.

Yours _____ (14),

*John King*

John King
Managing Director

---

**Exercise 2.4**
*Focus on punctuation*

What is the name for these punctuation marks?
Match the punctuation mark with its name.
The names are not in the correct order.

.  ,  ;  :  -  ( )  —  " "  ' '  '  !  ?

comma, full stop (US period), question mark, dash, colon, semi-colon, hyphen, apostrophe, inverted commas (single and double), brackets (open and close), exclamation mark (US exclamation point)

## UNIT TWO

These signs are often found in business documents.
Match the sign with its name.

%   @   *   /   &

asterisk, at, ampersand (said as 'and'), per cent, stroke or
oblique (US slant or slash)

Work with a partner.
Read these sentences aloud, making the punctuation clear.
Your partner should write them down.
For example: The words 'FRAGILE – HANDLE WITH
        CARE' should be stamped on every box.
        You say: The words open inverted commas
        capital letters FRAGILE dash HANDLE
        WITH CARE close inverted commas should be
        stamped on every box.

**a**   At the top of the letter it says 'HP Morris & Sons Ltd,
      Tel: 01 588 6213.'
**b**   The name on the box is 'John Smith (Chelsea) Ltd.'
**c**   Our reference is RB/12.
**d**   We ordered 20 boxes @ £3.75 each.
**e**   The letter is from Philip Carter-Brown.
**f**   We saw your advertisement in 'The Times'.
**g**   Mr Taylor's initials – JET – are on the receipt.
**h**   Mr Chevalier's telephone number is (33) 74 52 28 65 and
      Mr Chan Kam Hing's number is 3-7131605.
**i**   Please address the letter to:

Piovesan Silvana
Via Roma, no 27/a
31010 Salgareda (TV)
Italia

**Exercise 2.5**
***Listen to this:***
***Dictation practice***

You work in the purchasing department of Silver Office
Supplies Ltd, 14 North Street, London EC1 7AD. Your boss
Mr David Jackson, has recorded a letter for you to write.
First write the name and address of your company, then
listen to the cassette and write the letter.

# UNIT TWO

**Exercise 2.6**
*Letter writing*

You work for a German company that sells furniture –
Kurt Schiller Gmb H, Freidenstrasse 44, Hamburg, West
Germany.

Your are interested in importing hand-made sofa-beds from
the UK. You saw this advertisement in an English newspaper
'The Guardian'.

SOFASTASLEEP ON SOFA-BEDS HAND-MADE IN PINE
TO OUR OWN ORIGINAL DESIGN.

SEATS FOUR                    SLEEPS TWO

FOR AN ILLUSTRATED CATALOGUE OF OUR
COMPLETE RANGE OF HAND-MADE PINE
FURNITURE, WRITE TO:

THE NEW ART MANUFACTURING COMPANY LTD
96–98 WOOD LANE CHISWICK LONDON W5A 3EU

Write a letter of enquiry for Mr Johann Schmidt, the Sales
Manager, to sign.
Ask for catalogues, price lists and information about cash or
trade discounts.
Use the list of functions and the model letters to help you.

CHECKLIST: Make sure your letter has –

> **your company's name and address**
> **the recipient's name and address**
> **your reference**
> **date**
> **salutation**
> **first paragraph – say where you saw the advertisement**
> **second paragraph – give information about your**
>                          **company and reason for writing**
> **third paragraph – request action**
> **close**
> **ending**
> **signature, name and position in company**

# UNIT TWO

### Exercise 2.7
*Letter writing*

SEND FOR COLOUR BROCHURE:

**PROMADS LTD**
54 MANSELL STREET
SURBITON SURREY
KT6 7HO

To advertise their products companies often give away pens, T-shirts and other things with the company's name on them. What other things are given away for this purpose?

Your company, Modern Office Furniture, 36–42 Chaucer Road, London, SW4 6JZ, is interested in promotional advertising material to give to customers.

You saw this advertisement in this month's 'Campaign'. Mrs C Barlow, the manager, has asked you to draft a letter of enquiry (for her to sign) to Promads Ltd asking them to send you their colour brochure.
Use today's date and lay the letter out correctly.

### Exercise 2.8
*Advertising*

Companies can choose whether to advertise on television, in popular or quality newspapers, or in specialised magazines. Can you think of any other advertising media?
A company selling agricultural machinery, for example, will advertise in a farming magazine because in this way the advertisement will be seen by people who are likely to buy the product. It would be a waste of money to advertise agricultural machinery in a magazine for teenagers. To take another example, a company selling soap, which is used by everyone, will advertise on television because everyone watches television.
In the language of advertising, the group of people whom the advertiser is trying to reach is known as the 'target audience'. To get the most value for money, that is to be cost effective, it is necessary for advertisers to match the advertising medium to the target audience.
Where do you think would be the best place to advertise:

| | | |
|---|---|---|
| football boots | roof tiles | books |
| cosmetics | off-road vehicles | tents |
| soap powder | weedkiller | |

*Making comparisons*

Speedtel Ltd, a leading telecommunications company, sells its specialised products to businesses. It does not sell to the general public. Speedtel spent £150,000 on advertising last year.

28

## UNIT TWO

Study the pie chart to see how the money was spent.

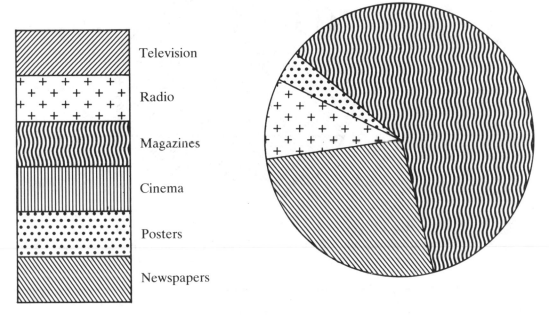

Television

Radio

Magazines

Cinema

Posters

Newspapers

**Exercise 2.9**
*Check your understanding*

a  Which advertising medium did they spend the least money on? Why?

b  Which advertising medium did they spend the most money on? Why?

c  Why did they spend more money on advertising in business magazines than on advertising in newspapers?

d  Why did they spend less money on radio advertising than on newspaper advertising?

**Exercise 2.10**
*Explaining what diagrams mean*

Chapmans Cameras Ltd sells photographic and electrical goods to the general public. It has a shop in every large town in the UK. It spent £250,000 on advertising last year.

Work with a partner.
Study the pie chart on page 30 and give a brief oral report on how the company spent the money.
Your partner should listen to your description and draw a rough pie chart, and afterwards look at the pie chart in the book.
Here are some expressions that you can use:
*The company advertised in . . . different media.*
*It spent most money, about . . . per cent, on . . .*
*It didn't spend a lot of money on . . . , only about . . . per cent.*
*It spent the same amount of money on . . . as on . . .*

29

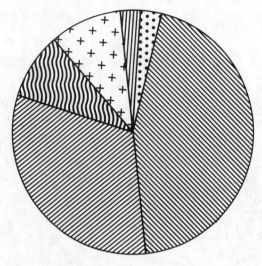

**Exercise 2.11**
*Writing a memo*

One of your colleagues has shown you a rough draft for his report on the advertising expenditure of Chapmans Cameras Ltd. However, he has not understood the information in the pie chart. Re-write his report, putting right the mistakes he has made.

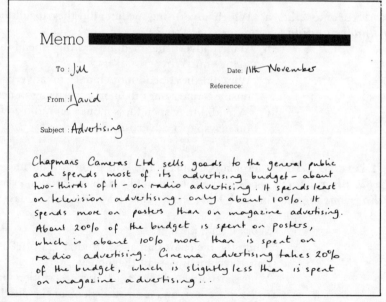

Memo ████████████████████████████

To : Jill                    Date: 11th November

                             Reference:

From : David

Subject : Advertising

Chapmans Cameras Ltd sells goods to the general public and spends most of its advertising budget - about two-thirds of it - on radio advertising. It spends least on television advertising - only about 10%. It spends more on posters than on magazine advertising. About 20% of the budget is spent on posters, which is about 10% more than is spent on radio advertising. Cinema advertising takes 20% of the budget, which is slightly less than is spent on magazine advertising...

 **Exercise 2.12**
*Listen to this*

Listen to this part of Graham Forbes's interview with Paul Barton, who explains what products are sold by Chapmans Cameras Ltd.
Draw a pie chart to illustrate the information that Paul Barton gives. Your pie chart will show the comparative sales figures of various goods.

## UNIT TWO

**Exercise 2.13**
*How to say it: Dates*

Note carefully from the examples how to say these dates.

| YOU WRITE IT LIKE THIS | YOU SAY IT LIKE THIS |
|---|---|
| 1st January 1986 | the first of January nineteen eighty-six |
| 2nd March 1987 | the second of March nineteen eighty-seven |
| 23rd May 2001 | the twenty-third of May two thousand and one |
| 17th June 1900 | the seventeenth of June nineteen hundred |
| 5th August 1989 | the fifth of August nineteen eighty-nine |
| 20th September 1990 | the twentieth of September nineteen-ninety |

Work with a partner.
One of you should read out these dates and the other should write them down.

| | |
|---|---|
| 21st February 1988 | 11th November 1918 |
| 22nd April 1990 | 14th July 1789 |
| 3rd July 1991 | 21st July 1969 |
| 13th October 1995 | 3rd January 1868 |
| 30th November 1989 | 29th May 1953 |

As you write down what your partner says, you might want to say:

*Could you say that again, please?*   *Just a minute, please.*
*Did you say eighty-eight?*   *Was that thirteen or thirty?*
*Shall I write it in figures or words?*   *Could you say it slowly, please?*

**Exercise 2.14**
*Listen to this:*
*Making notes of a discussion*

Read Sir John Apton's letter and listen to the informal meeting that took place at the advertising agency of McCann, Knott and Crocker to discuss the best way to advertise a fruit drink.

Make notes on these points:

**a**   the names of people present at the meeting
**b**   the purpose of the meeting
**c**   the product
**d**   the market share now
**e**   reasons for popularity
**f**   reason for advertising

## UNIT TWO

**g**  launch budget for advertising campaign
**h**  preparatory work
**i**  target audience
**j**  possible problems
**k**  date of visit to factory

**Exercise 2.15**
*Oral summary*
*and letter writing*

Using your notes:

**a**  Give an oral summary of the main points.
**b**  Complete the letter of enquiry from Sir John Apton.
**c**  Write a letter from Simon Crocker to Sir John Apton summarising the main points of the discussion. Don't include information that Sir John Apton knew before the meeting.

APTON
FRUIT DRINKS LTD

Chairman: Sir John Apton, MC, MBE

Registered Number: 811332 England
Registered Office: 1 Grieve Way, Taunton, Somerset TA5 6NG

Tel: 459376
Cables: APFRUIT
Telex: 753537

Pippin Way
Taunton
Somerset
TA5 2PW

McCann, Knott and Crocker
Marketing Solutions
2 Monmouth Row
London WC2 1AR

Our ref:  SJA/TP

30 June 19-

Dear Sirs

Your agency has been recommended to me by Mr Richard Grenville, Chairman
of Taunton Mills Ltd, for whom you developed a successful advertising
campaign last year.

My company, which has manufactured soft drinks since 1875, has recently
increased its production capacity and is now able to expand into the
national market.  The success of our new apple drink ................
....................................................................
....................................

I shall be in London from 14 to 17 July and therefore suggest that
we arrange a meeting at your office to discuss this matter further.

I look forward to meeting you.

Yours faithfully

*John Apton*

Sir John Apton

**Exercise 2.16**
*A letter from the USA*

Kurt Schiller Gmb H have received this letter from a furniture manufacturer in the USA.

**a** How does this letter differ from the British business letters that you have already read?

**b** Can you find any differences from British business letters in the vocabulary and spelling used in the body of the letter?

MAYFLOWER
Furniture Inc
1350 Atlantic Street
Springfields
Virginia 22151

Tel: (703) 523-1426
Cables: PILGRIM USA
Telex: 282429 MAYFL USA

Kurt Schiller GmbH
Freidensstr. 44
2000 Hamburg 50
West Germany

November 30, 19-

Gentlemen:

We are pleased to announce the arrival of our traditional American furniture on the European market.

The enclosed full-color pamphlet is designed to introduce you to our complete range, which includes such collectors' pieces as "The Old Kentucky Rocking Chair". To fully appreciate the superior quality of our designs, materials and craftmanship, we cordially invite you to our special exhibition at the Schloss Hotel, Lindenstrasse, Hamburg, open daily, 11 a.m. to 8 p.m., December 5-12 inclusive.

We are sure a visit will be a good investment of your time. Call this toll-free number - 69 40 61 31 - for a courtesy car to pick you up at a time that suits you.

Very truly yours,

*Frank Bigelow Jr*

Frank Bigelow, Jr.
Marketing Controller (Europe)

fb/gk

Enc. pamphlet

# UNIT TWO

**Exercise 2.17**
*Making notes*

Read this passage and make notes on the different types of
business organisation in the United Kingdom.
Your notes should look like this:

| | |
|---|---|
| TYPE OF BUSINESS: | Sole Trader or Proprietor |
| NUMBER OF MEMBERS: | One |
| SOURCE OF CAPITAL: | Provided by owner |
| PROFIT: | Kept by owner |
| LEGAL REQUIREMENTS: | No special requirements – but name of business must be registered if different from owner's name |
| CONTROL: | Controlled by owner |
| LIABILITY: | Unlimited |
| COMMENTS: | A popular type of business for small shops, self employed craftsmen |

## Types of business organisation in the United Kingdom

We should ask ourselves the following questions when considering how types of companies differ.
*Where did the money to start or expand the business come from?*
*Who owns or controls the company?*
*What happens to the profit?*
*What legal requirements must the company satisfy?*
*Does the company have limited or unlimited liability\*?*

\* Unlimited liability means that if a business gets into debt and eventually fails then all the private wealth
of the owner(s) can be used to pay the creditors – the people the business owes money to. If a business has
limited liability and it fails, the owners lose only the money that they have invested in the company and no
more.

The simplest form of business organisation is the sole trader or SOLE PROPRIETOR – one person
who provides the capital (the money needed to start), has complete control of the business,
keeps all the profit (or bears the loss), and has unlimited liability. It is not necessary to publish
the accounts and there are no special legal requirements except that the name of the business
must be registered if it is different from the owner's name. It is easy to start this type of
business, but it can be difficult to compete with large firms, and difficult to raise money for
expansion. When people open small shops, or work for themselves as plumbers, decorators and
so on, they are usually sole proprietors. These are 'one-man businesses' but they can, of course,
employ others.

The amount of money available for investing in a business can be increased by forming a
PARTNERSHIP of at least two people, who all contribute capital to the business and share the
profit in agreed proportions. Like sole proprietors, partnerships have unlimited liability and
there are no special legal requirements. Professional people such as doctors, accountants and
solicitors often form partnerships.

PRIVATE LIMITED COMPANIES have at least two but usually not more than fifty members who provide the capital which is divided into shares. A private limited company is controlled by a Board of Directors elected by the shareholders – one share, one vote. Shares can be transferred only with the agreement of other shareholders and cannot be offered for sale to the general public. The profit is distributed to the shareholders in proportion to the number of shares they own. A private limited company has limited liability and this is indicated by the letters LTD after its name. There are several legal requirements, including the submission of a Memorandum of Association and other documents to the Registrar of Companies when the company is set up, and the publication of annual accounts. Many medium-sized companies in manufacturing and retailing are of this type. They do not usually become very large since they must obtain capital for expansion either from the profits or by borrowing from a bank.

Sometimes a private limited company becomes a PUBLIC LIMITED COMPANY – which must put the letters PLC after its name. A PLC has at least two members but no maximum since it can offer its shares for sale to the public and may, therefore, have hundreds of thousands of shareholders, who have one vote for each share they own. Like private limited companies, PLCs have limited liability, must have a Memorandum of Association, publish their accounts and are subject to many legal requirements as set out in the Companies Act, 1985. The shareholders are the owners of the company and elect the Board of Directors who control it. Shareholders cannot sell their shares back to the company but they can sell their shares to people who wish to buy on the Stock Exchange (see Unit Eleven). The price of shares will go up if the PLC is making good profits and will go down if it is not doing so well. That part of the profit which is not re-invested in the company is paid out to shareholders as a dividend (e.g. 6p per share). It is possible for anyone who succeeds in buying 51% of the shares to gain control of a PLC.

**Exercise 2.18**    In addition to the types of business mentioned, there are also NATIONALISED INDUSTRIES, CO-OPERATIVES and FRANCHISES.

Can you identify examples of these in Britain or your country and explain how they operate?

## The City of London

When we talk about 'the City of London', we do not mean London, the capital of England. The phrase 'the City of London' refers to a small part of London, slightly east of the centre, where there is a concentration of banks, insurance companies and financial markets. Half a million people work in this area, but only about 5,000 live there.

It was the Romans who, shortly after the invasion of Britain ordered by the Emperor Claudius in 43 A.D., founded London. They built a bridge over the River Thames and a town developed around the northern end of the bridge. Eventually, the Romans built a wall around London (parts of it still exist) and the line of this wall roughly marks the area we call the City of London, now only a small part of the entire city. Roman London was a large and important centre of trade, but when the Roman legions left Britain in 409 A.D., it went into decline. The Anglo-Saxon settlers who came to England from North-West Europe between 400 and 600 A.D. did not live in the Roman cities but in villages outside them. However, in the ninth century, the Anglo-Saxon king, Alfred the Great, recognised the importance of London as a bastion against Viking attacks, and London once again developed into an important military and commercial centre. When William of Normandy invaded England and became king in 1066, London was the most important city in England.

By the twelfth century, there were two cities in the area we now call London – the City of London, associated with financial and commercial activities, and, further along the river to the west, the City of Westminster, associated with the king, government, parliament and the church. In this area today are situated the Houses of Parliament, Westminster Abbey, 10 Downing Street and most government offices. In the medieval period, the two cities were physically separate, with green fields in between. Relations between the two cities were not always good, partly because the king was often heavily in debt to city financiers. The City of London had its own elected mayor, known as the Lord Mayor from 1414, and the king or queen of England could not enter the City of London without the Lord Mayor's permission.

In the thirteenth century, Lombard bankers from Northern Italy played an important part in the development of banking services in the City of London. There is still a street there today called 'Lombard Street'. It was City financiers who provided the backing for the voyages of discovery in the sixteenth and seventeenth centuries. Ships sailed to the Americas, Asia and Africa to trade in tobacco, sugar, spices, gold and slaves. If they returned, then the profits from the sale of the cargo were shared out amongst those who had financed the voyage. These men were known as Merchant Venturers. Several of the major financial institutions of today can trace their origins back to the seventeenth century.

**Exercise 2.19**
*Things to find out*

Find out about one of these topics. Report what you have learnt in writing or as a short talk.

| | | | |
|---|---|---|---|
| **a** | Roman Britain | **d** | The Lombard Bankers |
| **b** | Alfred the Great | **e** | The Voyages of Discovery |
| **c** | William of Normandy | **f** | The economic history of your own town or city |

# UNIT THREE

In this unit you will learn how to reply to some of the letters of enquiry that you studied in Unit Two.

**Exercise 3.1**  Here is the reply to the letter from Mr Evans of Motofleet Hire plc.

Read it carefully and answer the questions that follow.

---

# ≡SPEEDTEL≡

Speedtel plc
70 Bush Lane
Epsom
Surrey
EL3 4TW

Tel: 0372 4343
Cables: SPEEDTEL
Telex: 546876 SPEED G

Registered Number: 2334121 England
Registered Office: 70 Bush Lane, Epsom, Surrey EL3 4TW

Mr D Evans
Managing Director
Motofleet Hire plc
Fleet House
1 London Road
Winchester
Wiltshire
WN1 2TS

Your ref:  DE/ts
Our ref:   JB/12

4 February 19–

Dear Mr Evans

We thank you for your letter of 2 February 19–, in which you enquired about our Autocomm car phone.

We enclose our latest catalogue and price list and we are sending the promotional video film which you requested under separate cover. We can quote you a discount of 10% for orders over a hundred, increasing to 15% on orders over two hundred.

Our promotional film provides an informative introduction to the 'Autocomm', but we would like to suggest that one of our representatives should visit you to demonstrate the exceptional quality of our product. Please do not hesitate to contact us to arrange a suitable date and time for a demonstration.

Yours sincerely

*Joanne Browning*

Joanne Browning (Mrs)
Senior Sales Manager

---

# UNIT THREE

*Check your understanding*
**a** What does 'Your ref: DE/ts' mean?
**b** Why does the letter end 'Yours sincerely'?
**c** Why do you think the video film has been sent separately?
**d** Now read the letter again. Then close your book and give an oral summary of the letter (see page 23 for useful expressions).

*Focus on functions:*
*How should you reply to a*
*letter of enquiry?*

**1** Acknowledge the letter.
**2** State what action you are taking.
**3** Focus attention on important information.
**4** Answer any specific questions the enquirer asked, for example about prices and delivery.
**5** Suggest ways in which you could help the enquirer to make a decision to buy.
**6** Invite the enquirer to ask for further information.
**7** Close the letter and add the appropriate ending.

**A** Match the sentences in Joanne Browning's letter with the functions listed above.
E.g. 6 Invite the enquirer to ask for further information.
'Please do not hesitate to contact us to arrange a suitable date and time for a demonstration.'

**B** Match the sentences below with the list of functions.
E.g. 1 Acknowledge the letter.
j Thank you for your letter of 1 March requesting information about . . .
Some functions can be matched with more than one sentence.
**a** If you wish we can arrange for a demonstration by . . .
**b** Please note that we are offering a 12½% trade discount.
**c** We are sending the samples you requested under separate cover.
**d** We thank you for your letter of 2 May enquiring about. . .
**e** Please do not hesitate to contact us if you would like any further information.
**f** Our prices include insurance and delivery.
**g** We have pleasure in enclosing our latest catalogue and price list.
**h** If you would like any further information, please do not hesitate to contact us.
**i** We are glad to be able to inform you that we are able to deliver from stock.
**j** Thank you for your letter of 1 March requesting information about . . .
**k** We would like to draw your attention to our offer of . . .
**l** We would like to suggest a demonstration of this model by one of our representatives.

**C** Work with a partner. Student A should describe how to reply to enquiries. Use these words: First of all, After that, Next, Then, To end with.
E.g. 'First of all, you should acknowledge the letter . . .'
Student B should check what A says be looking at the list of functions.

**Exercise 3.2** Complete this letter. Refer to the list of functions on page 38 to help you.

---

# SHIPTONS

Shiptons Cross Country Vehicles Ltd
359 Mottingham Road
Greenwich
London SE10 2AF

Tel: 01 305 7878
Cables: CROSCO
Telex: 342235 SHIPCRO G

Registered Office: 5 South Street, London SE10 3BT
Registered in England: No 567899

Mr J King
Managing Director
Across Africa Safaris Ltd
Standard Street
PO Box 49420
Nairobi
Kenya

Your ref: JK/kl
Our ref: GA/rt

10 April 19—

Dear Mr King

Thank you _____ (1) your letter _____ (2) 5 April enquiring _____ (3) our Ranger vehicles.

We _____ (4) pleasure _____ (5) enclosing our latest brochures and price list.  Please _____ (6) that the prices quoted do not _____ (7) insurance and delivery.

As we _____ (8) received a large number of _____ (9) from all over East Africa in response to our advertisement, we _____ (10) shipping two of our _____ (11) to Nairobi, and sending out _____ (12) of our most experienced _____ (13).

We _____ (14) that you should contact Mr Alan Munro, who will be staying _____.(15) the Metropolitan Hotel, Nairobi, between 9 and 30 June, if you _____ (16) like to examine and drive these vehicles.  The Ranger vehicles that we are sending out _____ (17) special modifications, carried out by ourselves, which will be of particular _____ (18) to you.

We look _____ (19) to hearing from you.

Yours _____ (20)

George Armstrong
Sales Manager

Enc.  brochures and price list

# UNIT THREE

**Exercise 3.3**
*Focus on punctuation:*
*The comma – part one*

Notice how commas are used in these sentences:

a   We enclose our latest catalogue and price list, and the promotional film is being sent under separate cover.

b   Our video film provides an informative introduction to the Autocomm, but we would like to suggest that one of our representatives pays you a visit.

BUT

c   We have sent them our current brochure and full details of our special offer.

WHAT IS THE DIFFERENCE? WHY ARE THEY DIFFERENT?

Punctuate these sentences.

d   we saw the training film and it seemed suitable for use on our secretarial course

e   we checked the case but not the goods inside

f   we have received your catalogue and price list but the promotional film has not yet arrived

g   here are the details of the new models and the revised prices

h   the company provides you with a car and full insurance cover but you must purchase your own petrol

**Exercise 3.4**
*Listen to this:*
*Dictation practice*

You work in the export sales department of Shonan Computers, 1–33 Kitashinjuku 7-chome, Shinjuku-ku, Tokyo 160, Japan. Mr Akira Suzuki, the Sales Manager, has received a letter from Silver Office Supplies Ltd. He has recorded his reply for you to write. First, write the name and address of your company and then listen to the cassette and write the letter.

**Exercise 3.5**
*Letter writing*

Georgina Dickenson, Managing Director of The New Art Manufacturing Company Ltd, has asked you to write a reply to the letter of enquiry from the German furniture retailer, Kurt Schiller (see page 27).
Prepare a letter for Ms Dickenson's signature.

CHECKLIST: Make sure your letter has –

**your company's name and address**
**recipient's name and address**
**Your ref/Our ref**
**date**

# UNIT THREE

salutation
paragraph one – acknowledge letter of enquiry
paragraph two – refer to catalogue and price list
                  mention discounts
paragraph three – invite request for further information
close
ending
signature
name
position in company
enclosures


**Price quotations in international trade**

In their reply to Mr King, Shiptons Cross Country Vehicles said 'Please note that the prices quoted do not include insurance and delivery'.

In international trade a seller will charge different prices according to the services they provide to the buyer. If the buyer collects the goods from the seller's address, the price will be much lower than if the seller delivers to the buyer's address. The costs that have to be considered are:

the goods themselves
transport
insurance.

Some of the standard price terms used in international trade are described in the table below.

Study it carefully and answer the questions that follow.

| SHIPPING TERMS | ABBREVIATION | WHAT THE PRICE INCLUDES |
| --- | --- | --- |
| Ex-works | EXW | Goods and packaging only – buyer collects from seller's address |
| Free on Board | FOB | All costs up to loading the goods on board a ship or aircraft but not the cost of transport |
| Free Carrier | FRC | All costs up to delivery to a carrier at a named point. Commonly used for container traffic. |

| Cost and Freight | C & F | All costs except insurance up to port of destination |
| Cost, Insurance and Freight | CIF | All costs including insurance up to port of destination |
| Delivered Duty Paid | DDP | Insured delivery including duty to the buyer's address |

What do you think these shipping terms mean?
FAS
FOR
FOT
FOA
DCP
CIP

**Exercise 3.6**
*Check your understanding*

Are the following statements TRUE or FALSE?

a If the buyers pay the DDP price, they don't have to pay anything more for transport and insurance.
b The FOB price will be higher than the CIF price.
c If the buyers pay the CIF price, they will not have to arrange any transport for the goods.
d If the exporters sell at the FRC price, they don't have to pay for the goods to be loaded onto the ship.
e If the price is C & F, the buyers must arrange insurance themselves.

**Exercise 3.7**
*Say what you think would happen in these situations*

a Atkins & Sons Ltd, of Manchester, England, wish to order a consignment of shoes from Singapore. An ex-works price of £20,000 has been quoted. If they accept this, what must they then do?
b Elextron Ltd, a small company in Aberdeen, Scotland, wishes to buy some specialised electrical equipment from a company in Canada. Elextron has not imported before. Which price quotation are they likely to choose?
c Maplin plc is a large importer of agricultural machinery and is able to obtain discounts on shipping and insurance charges. Which price quotation are they likely to choose?

## UNIT THREE

**Exercise 3.8**
*Completing a
short report*

You work for Silver Office Supplies Ltd, in London.
Your company wishes to import 600 word processors from
Shonan Computers, Tokyo, Japan. You have on your desk
information about price quotations, and costs of transport
and insurance.
Study this information with a partner. Then complete the
short report to your manager recommending the cheapest
way to buy.

---

### SHONAN COMPUTERS K. K.

PRICE LIST: valid up to and including 30th May 19—
MODEL: SCROLL 2000 WORD PROCESSOR (including printer)
SHIPPING TERMS: for 600 units

| | |
|---|---|
| Ex works: | £154,000 |
| FOB Yokohama | £155,000 |
| CIF Southampton | £168,000 |
| DDP SOS office London | £170,000 |

---

### ———————— Memo ————————

To : *Barry*                   Date:

                               Reference:

From : *John*

Subject :

Here is the information you required about the Red Funnel
Line's shipping services Yokohama – Southampton:
£14,000 for our cargo of word processors
plus £2,000 all-risks insurance.

I also checked the rail charges for this order:

British Rail Southampton – London (including insurance)
£1,000 (plus lorry to warehouse – use our own vans?)
I got a quotation from Moveright Road Services – £900 from
Southampton Docks to our London warehouse plus insurance
at £1 for every £100 value of cargo.

Do you need any more information?

---

# Memo ████████████████████████████████

To :                                                     Date:

From :                                                   Reference:

Subject :

```
If we _____(1) these goods C I F Southampton, we will have to pay _____(2)
to Shonan plus _____(3) costs of £1,000 for _____(4) freight, which _____(5)
insurance, making a total cost of _____(6).

This will be _____(7) than the _____(8) price of £170,000 and cheaper than
the F O B Yokohama price, which, with _____(9) costs, will come to £171,000
just to get the goods to Southampton.

I _____(10) recommend that we purchase ...
```

---

**Exercise 3.9**
*Conditional sentences*
*Giving a short*
*spoken report*

If we order 500 machines, the discount will be 30%

It is unlikely that we can order more than 500, but could you tell us what the discount would be if we ordered 2,000?

If we had purchased FOB Yokohama instead of CIF Southampton we would have paid £3,000 more than we needed.

You have received the following note from Mr Jackson, the Chief Buyer.

---

JOHN

Please check the discounts on the scrollwrite discs,
and report to me in person— today if possible.
What is the discount on 100? on 200? and the
total cost?
If we buy 300, how much?
More than 300 is out of the question, but
check, in any case, the discounts on 500 and
1000 and the total cost.

DAVID

## UNIT THREE

Look at the details of discounts in the catalogue and prepare what you will say when you see Mr Jackson.

### WP SCROLLWRITE DISCS MP2

Unit price £4 each – supplied in boxes of 50

| QUANTITY | DISCOUNT |
|----------|----------|
| up to    200 | nil |
| over     200 | 5% |
| over     300 | 10% |
| over     400 | 15% |
| over     500 | 20% |
| over    1000 | 25% |

**Exercise 3.10**
**Listen to this**

George Jackson sent Paula Armstrong to meet Murray Nixon, the London representative of Shonan Computers. He gave her a list of things he wanted her to find out about the Scroll 2000.

Listen to the conversation with Mr Nixon and make notes on the listed points.

After making your notes, you should write a report on the demonstration for Mr Jackson and be prepared to give an oral summary.

Meeting with Mr Nixon 21st February 10.30 am
Scroll 2000 demo

Points to check

a) What is included in price?
b) Guarantee?
c) Size / Weight?
d) Health dangers?
e) Foreign language keys?
f) Fragile?
g) Easy to use?

# UNIT THREE

**Exercise 3.11**
*Oral practice*

Study the following checklist and prepare to say why the other word processors you tested were not suitable.

| PRODUCT NAME: | WORDSURE | LOGOS 21 | STARKING | PALIMPSEST |
|---|---|---|---|---|
| PRICE : | O.K. | expensive | O.k. | O.k. |
| PRINTER : | too slow | not included in price | not very clear print | very noisy |
| KEYBOARD : | O.k. | O.k. | didn't have many functions | O.k. |
| SCREEN : | rather small | O.k. | O.k. | too bright no brightness control |

Work with a partner.
Continue this dialogue.

PAULA ARMSTRONG: I think we are going to order the SCROLL 2000.
COLLEAGUE: Did you consider purchasing the WORDSURE?
PAULA ARMSTRONG: We would have bought the WORDSURE if the screen had been bigger and the printer hadn't been so slow.
COLLEAGUE: What about . . .

**Exercise 3.12**
*How to say it*

This is how you ask about abbreviations:
*What does FOB stand for?*
*It stands for Free on Board.*
*And what does it mean?*
*It means that the price includes loading on to the ship but not the freight charge or insurance.*
Or sometimes like this:
*What does TUC stand for?*
*It stands for Trades Union Congress.*
*And what is that?*
*It is a central organisation to which British trade unions belong.*

## UNIT THREE

Work with a partner.
Ask what the following abbreviations stand for.
Your partner should look at the inside back cover of the book for the answers.

| | | | |
|---|---|---|---|
| EC | IMF | GMT | EFTA |
| UNO | EMS | CBI | BSI |
| OECD | CAP | GNP | DTI |
| CIF | VAT | DDP | ICC |
| ATM | FT | NCV | SITPRO |

Some abbreviations, especially names of organisations, are usually pronounced as words, and not as separate letters. For example:

UNESCO – United Nations Educational Scientific and
Cultural Organisation
GATT – General Agreement on Tariffs and Trade

Find out what these stand for. They are all to do with banking.

SWIFT          PIN          EFTPOS

**Exercise 3.13**
*Focus on vocabulary*

Choose one of these words or phrases to complete the sentences.
Write the sentences out in full.

    commercial invoice
    pro-forma invoice
    bill

**a** Because of the cold winter, our quarterly electricity _____ was higher than usual.

**b** Here is the _____ for the goods which arrived last week. It must be paid within thirty days.

**c** We need precise information about the price we will have to pay, so ask Shonan Computers to send us a _____ .

    estimate
    quotation
    discount
    special offer

**d** The builder has given us a rough _____ of £600 for this work, but it could well cost much more.

**e** Because of current fluctuations in the price of our raw materials, we cannot give a precise _____ for your order.

**f** During December there is a _____ of two weeks' holiday for the price of one.

**g** We offer a _____ of 15% on orders for over 500 units.

range     sample
line      example

**h** This is the best-selling _____ in the supermarket.

**i** The catalogue contains information about our full _____ of electrical goods.

**j** We are sending a(n) _____ under separate cover, so that you can examine the superior quality of our cloth.

**k** Here is a(n) _____ of the letter you have to write – just change the name, address and date.

## Methods of payment in international trade

In international trade buyers and sellers may be thousands of miles apart, may not know each other's reputation, goods may take months to arrive, and, in addition, there are problems caused by different legal systems and currencies. There are methods of payment which help to overcome these problems of time, distance and mistrust.

## Open Account trading

The exporter, when he receives an order, sends the goods and the invoice to the importer. When he receives the goods, the importer pays the exporter by transferring money to the exporter's bank account. An exporter will only do business in this way with long-standing and trustworthy customers. An exporter is unlikely to offer open account trading to a new customer. If the importer simply does not pay, there is little the exporter can do about it without going to a lot of trouble and inconvenience. However, this is a cheap and simple payment system for companies that have a good trading relationship.

*Check your understanding*

**a** What are the problems of payment in international trade?

**b** Does open account trading solve these problems?

**c** If the importer did not pay the invoice, what could the exporter do?

**d** What is the advantage of open account trading?

# UNIT THREE

**Bills of Exchange**

Bills of Exchange have been in use for hundreds of years. They enable the importer to receive and possibly sell the goods before he has to pay for them. They allow the exporter to be paid for the goods as soon as he has sent them to the importer. There are three parties to a bill.

the drawer – the company that prepares the bill and is owed money, that is the seller of the goods. His signature is on the bill.

the drawee – the company to whom the bill is sent and who will pay, that is, the buyer of the goods. He accepts the bill by signing it. Banks also accept bills on behalf of their customers.

the payee – the company to whom payment is made. Usually the same as the drawer.

This bill shows that Techno is exporting goods to Marlin.

---

EXCHANGE FOR £100,000                                            27th June 19–

AT ..60.days.after.sight............. PAY THIS..sole.... BILL OF EXCHANGE.................

TO THE ORDER OF.. ourselves................................................

One hundred thousand pounds sterling

VALUE..Goods.................................          WHICH PLACE TO ACCOUNT
                                                       FOR AND ON BEHALF OF
TO:...Marlin.Electronics....................           Techno Products plc

..Atlantic.Square.......................               30 Thorpe Way
   Toronto                                             Manchester
   Ontario Canada                                      U K
   M4V 2Z2                                             Signed: M Corbett

---

*Check your understanding*   **e**  Who has prepared this bill?
                             **f**  Who will pay £100,000?
                             **g**  Has the buyer accepted this bill yet?
                             **h**  How long has the buyer got to pay?

If Techno do not want to wait sixty days to be paid, they can sell the bill at a discount to a specialist bank. Techno will receive slightly less than the full amount immediately, and the bank will keep the bill until it is time for it to be paid in full, or sell it to another bank.

*Check your understanding*   **i**  Why might Techno want to have the money immediately?
                             **j**  If a bank buys the bill from Techno, how will it make a profit?

# UNIT THREE

**Documentary collections**

In this system of payment the documents proving ownership of the goods are given to the importer only when he pays the Bill of Exchange. This is called Documents against Payment. Alternatively, the documents are handed over when the importer accepts the Bill of Exchange, that is agrees to pay after, say, 60 days. This is called Documents against Acceptance. The exporter uses a bank in the importer's country to make these arrangements. Study the diagram to see how this system works.

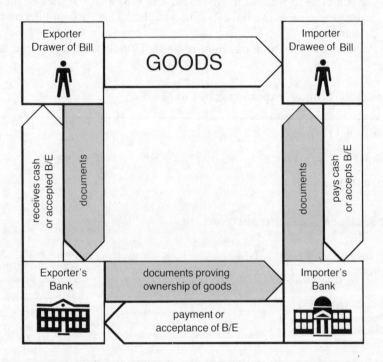

**Documentary credits**

Bills of Exchange are not entirely safe from the exporter's point of view because it is possible for the importer to refuse to pay. Because of this, the Documentary Credit system has developed. In this system, a bank guarantees to pay the exporter if the importer does not pay. In this type of transaction, Bills of Exchange are drawn on a bank. Documentary Credits are explained in detail in Unit Four.

What are the differences between this Bill of Exchange and the one on page 49?

```
EXCHANGE FOR £50,000                                    30th August 19-

AT..sight...............................  PAY THIS..sole... BILL OF EXCHANGE.................

TO THE ORDER OF  .ourselves..............................................................

     Fifty thousand pounds sterling

Drawn under irrevocable documentary credit no. 15249 dated 1st August 19-...

VALUE..goods..............................  WHICH PLACE TO ACCOUNT
                                            FOR AND ON BEHALF OF
TO:.Finlays Bank International...........   Techno Products plc
    32 Moor Street                          30 Thorpe Way
    London EC3...........................   Manchester
                                            U K
                                            Signed: M Corbett
```

## The City of London

In medieval times, the City of London was a centre of manufacturing and trade, and this is still reflected in the names of the streets today. There are street names such as 'Threadneedle Street' (where the tailors worked), 'Bread Street' (where the bakers were), 'Egg Street', 'Poultry', 'Cornhill', 'Shoe Lane', and so on. However, the City of London gradually became a supplier of financial services, not a place where goods were manufactured and traded. Overseas trade was very important in the development of the City's financial services. Indeed, it was far more important than domestic trade. The City played a very small part in the Industrial Revolution, which began in the North of England in the eighteenth century, and was financed by local banks, but it played a major part in the commercial life of the British Empire. By the nineteenth century 'the Bill on London', ie a Bill of Exchange drawn on a London bank was the common currency of international trade.

In the twentieth century, the City of London has become comparatively less important in world trade than it was in the nineteenth, and has to compete with cities which now have larger financial markets, such as New York and Tokyo. Nevertheless, it still remains a major international financial centre.

In the small area of the City, about one square mile, are grouped together the Bank of England, the head offices of 'the big four' clearing banks (Barclays, National Westminster, Lloyds and Midland), merchant banks, the head offices of major insurance companies, the Baltic Exchange, which provides shipping services, Lloyds of London – the famous insurance market, the Stock Exchange, where shares are bought and sold, and several commodity markets. In addition, there are over four hundred different foreign banks in the City. In fact, there are more United States banks in London than there are in New York.

The importance of the City of London lies in the international nature of its business. The banking, insurance, investment and shipping services it provides to the world are an important source of invisible earnings for the United Kingdom.

National Westminster Bank

Lloyds Bank

Bank of America

Midland Bank

 CREDIT SUISSE

HongkongBank

 CREDIT LYONNAIS

**Exercise 3.14**
*Things to find out*

Prepare and give a short talk on one of the following subjects:

a  The Industrial Revolution
b  The City of London in the nineteenth century
c  The history of another international financial centre, eg New York, Tokyo, Zurich, Frankfurt, Paris, Hong Kong, Singapore, Amsterdam, Milan

# UNIT FOUR *Revision and consolidation*

In this first revision unit you will practise the three types of letter that you have learned how to write: job applications, enquiry letters and replies to enquiry letters, as well as making notes and oral summaries.

**Exercise 4.1**
*Letter writing*

Read the letter that Malcolm Clarke wrote to his Uncle Charles and select information from it to write Malcolm's letter of application for the job advertised. Remember that the letter you write must be like the ones you studied in Unit One, not like Malcolm's letter to his uncle. Can you identify at least three characteristics of this letter which you would NOT include in a letter applying for a job?

15 College Road
Maldon
Sussex
CH4 5TG

Dear Uncle Charles,                                        14th October 19—

Thanks for your letter and for the cheque you sent me for my 21st birthday. I used it to buy myself a new suit.

Quite a lot of things have happened since I last saw you. Remember that job I had with the travel agency? Well, I gave it up six months ago. I couldn't see much of a future in it – a dead-end job really. The only thing I liked about it was all those trips to Spain – my Spanish really improved a lot. I'm working now for a company that sells kitchens (it's called "Beeton Kitchen Designs" – perhaps you've heard of it). I have to visit people's houses, measure up, sell them the right sort of kitchen units, and so on. The pay is good, but it's very hard work and I'm not sure it's what I really want to do.

Did I tell you that Sarah is doing the same college course that I did – you know, the one on Business and Computing at Maldon College? I hope she gets as much out of it as I did. I'm glad to hear that you like your new job in Toronto. If I were still working for the travel agency, I could get a cheap ticket and come over and see you, but as it is. . . . . . . . . . . . . . . . .

Seriously though, could you give me some advice about getting a job in Canada? I know I've had two jobs since I left college a year ago (three if you count the holiday job in the menswear shop) but I still haven't found something I really like.

Hope to hear from you soon

Yours,

Mal

P.S. I've reached the semi-finals of the Sussex County Chess Championship! Wish me luck!

## TRAINEE MEDIA SALES EXECUTIVES

One of Europe's top publishing companies is recruiting young men and women (18–25) to sell advertising space on a range of top quality international magazines.

Our clients expect bright, articulate and enthusiastic candidates who are able to work as members of a team. Experience of working in a competitive business environment would be an advantage, as would fluency in a foreign language. Applicants should have a genuine desire to develop a long-term career in this rewarding field. Successful candidates will receive thorough training, as well as a good basic salary and generous commission.

Write with full details to:
**Paul Farran, Media Appointments,**
19 Addison Walk, London WC2 9NN

**Exercise 4.2**
*Letter writing*

You work for a garden design company in your country. You have read an article in an English gardening magazine which reminds you of a business card you were given at a trade fair recently.

You decide to write a letter enquiring about the possibility of importing garden tractors. Address your letter to Mr Williams.

**HERCULES**
**GARDEN MACHINES LTD**

**P. J. WILLIAMS**
Representative

12 ARGOS STREET
NEWPORT
GWENT
WALES

Tel: 0633 51243

THE PROFESSIONAL GARDENER     MARCH

...... but the model that performed best in our tests was the '*Titan*' tractor, made by *Hercules Garden Machines Ltd*. It was simple to operate, mechanically reliable and cut grass more efficiently than the other tractors we tested. We therefore recommend it as our 'Best Buy'.

# UNIT FOUR

## Exercise 4.3
### *Letter writing*

Importaciones Torrents S.A.
Rambla Nova 103
08050 Barcelona
España

Tlfn. 219 0055
Telex: 44673 IMPTOR E
Director: Enric Torrents

*Peter, please write a reply to Importaciones — for me to sign*

Ms Shirley Blake                                    Our ref:   PM/mf
Sales Director
Banner Tools plc
100 Faraday Street
Halifax
West Yorkshire
HA2 5KL
United Kingdom                                     16 May 19-

Dear Ms Blake

We have heard about your company and its range of products from the
British Chamber of Commerce office in Barcelona. *— good, send some more leaflets to BCC*

We are a company which imports tools for the industrial and do-it-
yourself markets, and we are particularly interested in your 'Beaver'
chain saw, model 220A.
                                         *— send technical manual*
Could you please send us the full technical specification for this
product?   We would also like to receive information about discounts,
*one year guarantee on chain, two years on other parts* guarantees and the supply of replacement parts.

We look forward to receiving your reply.          *up to 100 — nil*
                                          *supplied*   *101–200 — 10%*
Yours sincerely                           *from stock,*  *201–300 — 15%*
                                          *directly from us*  *301 + — 25%*

*Enric Torrents*

Enric Torrents
Director

*Don't forget to say that the price includes one spare chain and a Users' Handbook in five languages, inc. Spanish — and send our complete catalogue, they might be interested in our other products.*

## Exercise 4.4
### *Note taking and summary*

Read this newspaper article about people who have changed
their jobs and make notes with these headings:

NAME OF PERSON:

FIRST JOB(S):

WHY HE OR SHE CHANGED JOBS:

THE JOB HE OR SHE DOES NOW:

Then give an oral summary of the article, using your notes.

# Jobs for life?
# Not any more

Every year hundreds of thousands of people change their careers or update their skills. Engineers from the traditional manufacturing industries are retraining in computer engineering, and more people are starting their own business.

A dramatic change was made recently by boxer Barry McGuigan, ex-featherweight champion of the world, who is giving up boxing to present programmes on BBC television. 'It'll be a lot easier on the face,' he explained.

Chris Tipping studied economics at Cambridge, considered working in a government office but then decided to make singing – his great love – his career. For five years he sang with the Westminster Abbey Choir and the BBC Singers. However, finding it difficult to make enough money to support his family – he was married with two children – he became an assistant to a Member of Parliament. In this job he had to deal with many legal and tax problems and eventually decided to become a lawyer himself. Although he had to study for four or five hours every evening after work, he has no regrets. He is now working as a lawyer in an office only two minutes from Westminster Abbey, where he still sings at weekends.

David Robinson, 37, started life as a music teacher. He noticed that musicians often suffered from bad necks and backs, caused by sitting for long periods on uncomfortable chairs. After twelve years as a teacher he turned to selling furniture designed for healthy sitting. His company, 'Alternative Sitting', is doing well. 'It started as a hobby,' he said, 'rather than a conscious pre-planned decision. I needed a change and the stimulus of running my own business.'

Barbara Winton left the world of business. She started as a jewellery designer, did a secretarial course, became a secretary and moved, for a high salary, to an oil company, where she became a senior administrator. After two years she left. 'I couldn't stand the falseness, selfishness and over-competitiveness of commerce,' she said, and now works as a homeopath, having completed a four-year course at the London College of Homeopathy.

**Exercise 4.5**
*Check your vocabulary*

Read the following passage and choose an appropriate word or phrase from the list to complete the sentences. Each word or phrase should be used once.

There are various ways of answering an _____ (1) for a job. You may be instructed to phone to arrange an _____ (2), obtain f _____ d _____ (3) and/or an a _____ f _____ (4). Alternatively, you may be instructed to send a full c _____ v _____ (5) which should be accompanied by a c _____ l _____ (6), or to write a full l _____ of a _____ (7).

## UNIT FOUR

Whichever method is used, it is essential that prospective a _____ (8) should read the advertisement very carefully to ensure that they fully understand the type of e _____ (9), skills and p _____ q _____ (10) the employer requires. Prospective applicants should also note the d _____ (11) which they will have to perform, as well as the w _____ e _____ (12), salary, general conditions and c _____ p _____ (13) which the job offers.

They should then consider carefully if the job is suitable for them and they are suitable for the job, comparing their previous experience and p _____ t _____ (14) with the r _____ (15) of the job, and also taking into account their future a _____ (16).

| | | |
|---|---|---|
| curriculum vitae | personal qualities | interview |
| advertisement | professional training | requirements |
| applicants | further details | experience |
| ambitions | letter of application | duties |
| career prospects | covering letter | |
| working environment | | |
| application form | | |

**Exercise 4.6**
*Check your vocabulary*

Find a word or phrase from the list below which matches the definitions given.

**a**  a percentage reduction in price
**b**  a book in which goods are listed and described
**c**  newspapers, radio and television
**d**  to put a product on the market
**e**  people who are expected to take notice of an advertisement
**f**  amount of money available for a certain purpose
**g**  a company that prepares advertisements for other companies
**h**  small items, often given away, that have the company's name on them

| | |
|---|---|
| promotional material | a catalogue |
| a budget | the target audience |
| a discount | the media |
| to launch | an advertising agency |

# UNIT FIVE

**Exercise 5.1**   In this letter Silver Office Supplies places an order with Shonan Computers. Read the letter and answer the questions that follow.

Silver Office Supplies Ltd
14 North Street
London
EC1 7AD

Tel: 01 280 4868
Cables: SOSUP
Telex: 934518 SILVOS G

Registered Number: 7713455 England
Registered Office: 3 Newcastle Street, London NW1 2AA

Mr A Suzuki
Sales Manager
Shonan Computers
1-33 Kitashinjuku 7-chome
Shinjuku-ku
Tokyo 160
Japan

Your ref:   AS/tg
Our ref:   DJ/wd

5 February 19-

Dear Mr Suzuki

Order for the SCROLL 2000 word processor

We thank you for your letter of 17 January, in which you enclosed your catalogue and price list, together with the booklet on the SCROLL 2000 word processor.

We have contacted Mr Nixon, as you suggested, and his demonstration of the SCROLL 2000 convinced us that this model will meet our requirements.  Your offer of a 20% trade discount, with a further discount for bulk orders, is also quite satisfactory.

We are therefore placing an order for 600 SCROLL 2000 word processors.  We enclose our official order form No.YT 945.

We discussed terms of payment with Mr Nixon and would like to confirm that payment is to be made by Documentary Credit.  Our bank will issue a Documentary Credit in your favour CIF Southampton.  You will be informed, through your own bank, of the type and number of documents that you must prepare.

Delivery by 30 April is essential, and we reserve the right to cancel the order and/or return the shipment at your risk and expense at any time after that date.

We look forward to receiving the shipment and doing business with you in future.

Yours sincerely

*David Jackson.*

David Jackson
Chief Buyer

Enc.   Order Form

# UNIT FIVE

**Check your understanding**

a How has Mr Jackson drawn attention to the subject of the letter?

b In his last letter to Shonan Computers (on page 26), Mr Jackson ended with 'Yours faithfully'. Why has he changed to using 'Yours sincerely'?

c Why have Shonan Computers offered a discount?

d If the goods arrive in Southampton on 30 April, have Silver Office Supplies got the right to return them?

e Why didn't Mr Jackson just send the order form without an accompanying letter?

f Close your book. Give an oral summary of the letter.

Here are some more useful expressions (also see page 23).

*He thanks us for sending* . . .      *He confirms that* . . .
*He refers to his meeting with* . . .      *He says that our bank will* . . .
*He encloses* . . .      *He makes it clear that delivery* . . .

**Focus on functions: What should you say in an order letter?**

1 Acknowledge previous correspondence.
2 State your reactions to the prices, discounts, samples etc.
3 Place the order.
4 Confirm terms of payment OR suggest terms of payment.
5 Set deadline for delivery (if appropriate).
6 Close the letter and add a formal ending.

A Match the sentences in David Jackson's letter with the functions listed above.

B Match the sentences below with the list of functions.

a Delivery before 5 May is a firm condition of the order.

b We thank you for your letter of 3 April quoting prices and delivery terms for . . .

c We are therefore ordering . . .

d We look forward to receiving our order and doing business with you in future.

e We are satisfied that the quoted terms are acceptable.

f As agreed, payment is to be made by Documentary Credit.

g We thank you for your letter of 1 March enclosing . . .

h We therefore enclose our official order form, No 41, for . . .

i We have examined the samples and are satisfied with their quality.

j Our usual method of payment is by . . . and we trust that this will be acceptable to you.

k We thank you for the samples/price list/catalogue which you sent us.

l We have tested the samples and are satisfied with their performance.

**Exercise 5.2**  Complete this letter.

KURT SCHILLER GmbH

Freidensstr. 44
2000 Hamburg 50
Tel: 69 43 02 11  Telex: 5216678 KSCH D

Ms G Dickenson                               Your ref:
Sales Manager                                Our ref:
The New Art Manufacturing Company Ltd
96-98 Wood Lane
Chiswick
London W5 2CB
United Kingdom                               9 May 19-

Dear Ms Dickenson

We _____(1) you _____(2) your letter of 2 May, in _____(3) you enclosed
your _____(4) price list and _____(5).

We are _____(6) that the _____(7) terms, including a 15% trade _____(8),
are acceptable, and our visit to your display at the Munich Furniture
Fair _____(9) us that the sofa-beds will _____(10) our requirements.

We therefore _____(11) our official _____(12) form, No. 2401, _____(13)
sixteen sofa-beds.

As this is the first time we have _____(14) business, we _____(15) that
payment should be by Documentary Credit.  We will instruct our bank to
_____(16) a Documentary Credit in your _____(17).  The terms are CIF
Hamburg, and your own bank will inform you of the _____(18) and _____(19)
of documents required.

This order is subject to delivery before 31 July, and we reserve the
_____(20) to cancel the order and/or _____(21) the goods at your own risk
and _____(22) at any time after that _____(23).

We look forward to _____(24) our order and doing further business with
you in future.

Yours _____(25)

J Schmidt
Chief Buyer


Enc. _____(26)

**Exercise 5.3**
*Focus on punctuation:*
*The comma – part two*

Notice how commas are used in these sentences:

a   We have ordered a dozen desks, a dozen swivel chairs, a dozen word processors and six filing cabinets.

b   We have received orders from NBA Ltd, P Carter and Sons, Sun Laboratories, Smart and Hoggett, and Aquaproof Ltd.

How many companies are listed in sentence B. If there were no comma in front of 'and', why might there be a problem?

Now punctuate these sentences.

c   send copies of this memo to mr dryden mr shelley mrs browning and miss radcliffe

d   we supply hammers drills ladders pumps and welding equipment

e   the opening ceremony was attended by lord cromwell lady ormsby sir william and lady alice harpur and colonel and mrs hardcastle

f   we promise to give you fast service the finest products full value for money and our very best work

g   please ask the library to order computers now management and training review and modern business practices

**Exercise 5.4**
*Listen to this:*
*Dictation practice*

You work in the purchasing department of Silver Office Supplies Ltd, 14 North Street, London EC1 7AD. Your boss, Mr David Jackson, has recorded a letter for you to prepare for his signature.
First, write the name and address of your company. Then listen to the cassette and write the letter.

**Exercise 5.5**
*Letter writing*

Mr J King, the Managing Director of Across Africa Safaris Ltd, wishes to order twelve Ranger vehicles from Shiptons Cross Country Vehicles. He has asked you to draft the order letter.
Use the model letters and the list of functions to help you.

CHECKLIST: Make sure your letter has –

**your company's name and address**
**recipient's name and address**
**your reference**

**date**
**salutation**
**first paragraph – refer to previous correspondence**
**second paragraph – state reaction to prices and goods**
         **refer to Mr Munro**
**third paragraph – place order**
**fourth paragraph – mention terms of payment**
**fifth paragraph – set deadline for delivery**
**close**
**ending**
**signature**
**name**
**position in company**

 **Exercise 5.6**
*Listen to this*

Robert Hart, Manager of Marlin Electronics, has left a message on cassette for you.
Listen to what he says and write a letter for his signature.

*Check your understanding*

**a** Who will you address the letter to?
**b** What kind of letter is it?
**c** What is the name of the product?
**d** How will payment be made?
**e** Is the delivery date important?
**f** What will you say about Dave Smith?

**Exercise 5.7**
*How to say it*

Make sure you know how to say large numbers in English.
Read the following numbers aloud.

| | |
|---|---|
| 101 | one hundred and one (say 'n' for 'and') |
| 127 | one hundred and twenty-seven |
| 1,001 | one thousand and one |
| 1,248 | one thousand two hundred and forty-eight |
| 103,203 | one hundred and three thousand two hundred and three |
| 5,384,509 | five million three hundred and eighty-four thousand five hundred and nine |
| 10,351,123,001 | ten billion three hundred and fifty-one million one hundred and twenty-three thousand and one |

## UNIT FIVE

Work with a partner.
Say these sentences aloud and ask your partner to write them down.

**a**  We need 105 square metres of carpet for the office.
**b**  There were 164 applicants for the job.
**c**  The car costs £9,034.
**d**  The house was sold for £83,750.
**e**  The population of the United Kingdom is 57,300,029.
**f**  The total value of exports was £6, 896,000,000.
**g**  The total value of imports was £4,669,891,262.
**h**  The bank's profits rose to $54,000,000.
**i**  Losses of £177,500 in 1987 were turned into profits of £144,850 in 1988.

### Visible and invisible trade

In these two examples, which country is exporting and which country is importing?

1  A Japanese ship carries frozen lamb from New Zealand to Canada.
2  An Englishman on holiday in Italy buys a ticket for the opera.

Trade in tangible goods, such as cars, rice and oil, is known as visible trade. When Japan sells cars to another country that is a visible export for Japan and a visible import for the other country.

A comparison of total visible exports and total visible imports gives us the BALANCE OF TRADE for a particular country.

Trade figures for the United Kingdom: (February 1985)
Total value of goods exported:      £5,895,000,000
Total value of goods imported:      £5,453,000,000

The Balance of Trade is favourable for the United Kingdom. There is a surplus of £442,000,000.
If imports were higher than exports, the Balance of Trade would be unfavourable, there would be a deficit.

As well as trade in tangible goods, there is also the buying and selling of the financial and shipping services needed for international trade. This trade, which is in services, not tangible goods, is known as invisible trade. There are four main areas of invisible trade:

BANKING:      money paid to British banks by foreign
              companies for banking services counts as a
              British export

## UNIT FIVE

INSURANCE: money paid to British insurance companies by foreign companies also counts as a British export

SHIPPING: money paid for shipping services is an important source of invisible earnings for countries with large shipping fleets, such as Norway and Greece

TOURISM: the money spent by tourists counts as an export for the country where the money is spent. For example, when a British tourist spends money in Italy, that is an Italian export

Can you think of any other examples of invisible trade?

A comparison of total visible and invisible exports with total visible and invisible imports is known as the BALANCE OF PAYMENTS.

**Exercise 5.8**
*Check your understanding*

Look at these examples. Say whether they are examples of visible or invisible trade.
For which country are they exports, and for which country are they imports?

a   A British theatre company performs plays in Greece.
b   An English person buys an Italian car in England.
c   An Italian working in England buys an Italian car in England.
d   A German buys a ticket to watch an American band play in Germany.
e   An Englishman buys some olive oil in France and takes it back to England.
f   A Norwegian ship carries frozen lamb from New Zealand to England.
g   A Canadian ship-owner insures his ship in London.

 **Exercise 5.9**
*Listen to this*

Listen to the cassette and complete the following table:

| QUARTERLY TRADE FIGURES FOR THE UNITED KINGDOM | |
| --- | --- |
| VISIBLE IMPORTS: | £ |
| VISIBLE EXPORTS: | £ |
| BALANCE OF TRADE Surplus or Deficit: | £ |
| INVISIBLE EXPORTS: | £ |
| INVISIBLE IMPORTS: | £ |
| BALANCE OF PAYMENTS Surplus or Deficit: | £ |

# UNIT FIVE

 **Exercise 5.10**
**Listen to this**

Listen to the conversation between David Jackson and Sally Brown. He is checking some information about six items which are sold by Silver Office Supplies. He is making notes for a meeting he has to go to. Complete his notes.

NOTES :..........................................................................

| PRODUCT | NUMBER IN STOCK | COMMENTS |
|---------|-----------------|----------|
| P.A. Executive desk | 500 | adequate stock |

**Exercise 5.11**
**Present perfect and past tenses**
**Talking about what you have done and when you did it**

*I've already doubled the order for that item.*
*They haven't arrived yet.*
*We have already sold most of our stock.*
*I cancelled the order two days ago.*
*They promised to deliver on Tuesday, 20th January.*

Work in pairs.
Student A should read the information on this page and Student B should look at page 66.

David Jackson is going on a trip to Italy. He wants to check that Sally Brown has arranged everything:

a flight    c hired car      e publicity material
b hotel     d taxi to the airport

In addition, he wants to check that she has dealt with the following matters:

f Miss Jones's interview
g the meeting with Mr Wells
h the new floppy disks

i the demonstration of the new Mica photocopier
j the Health and Safety Inspector's visit

Imagine you are David Jackson. Ask Sally Brown about the things you want to know. Start with the following questions:

*Have you booked my flight to Rome?*
*Have you booked my hotel room and hired a car for me?*
*Have you told Mr Wells that I can't come to next week's meeting?*

Now ask about the other things.

## UNIT FIVE

Read this page from Sally Brown's diary.
Prepare to answer David Jackson's questions.
Here are some of the answers you will need.

*Yes, I have. I booked it on Tuesday. First class, Alitalia.*
*Yes, I have. I did it two days ago.*
*I haven't done that yet, I'm afraid.*

Look at the diary for the information you need to answer
your partner's other questions. On what day are David
Jackson and Sally Brown speaking?

| | |
|---|---|
| **Monday 18** | invite Miss Jones to interview on 27th ✓<br>arrange appt. with Mr Wells 3 pm 25th ✓ |
| **Tuesday 19** | book flight 1st class Alitalia ✓<br>postpone Miss Jones's interview ✓<br>cancel Mr W's appt. — not done<br>phone printers about brochures for Italy ✓ |
| **Wednesday 20** | Cancel order for XM floppy disks - order MP2 disks ✓<br>book hotel in Rome + hired car ✓<br>arrange collection from printers ✓ |
| **Thursday 21** | speak to typists about punctuality - not done<br>arrange visit by Health and Safety Inspector ✓<br>phone engineer about central heating - no answer |
| **Friday 22** | book taxi to airport for 9am Mon - do today<br>get Mr J's signature on all outstanding letters<br>and order forms - don't forget! |

# UNIT FIVE

**Documentary credit transactions**

Documentary Credits (or Letters of Credit) are a very important METHOD OF PAYMENT in international trade. They are normally IRREVOCABLE which means that they cannot be changed or cancelled without the agreement of all parties. In order to understand how they work you must first realise that there are four parties to a Documentary Credit transaction.

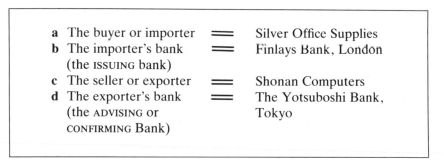

a  The buyer or importer  ===  Silver Office Supplies
b  The importer's bank  ===  Finlays Bank, London
   (the ISSUING bank)
c  The seller or exporter  ===  Shonan Computers
d  The exporter's bank  ===  The Yotsuboshi Bank,
   (the ADVISING or  Tokyo
   CONFIRMING Bank)

Firstly, the importer and the exporter must negotiate and agree a sales contract. Then the importer begins the Documentary Credit process by asking his bank to open a Documentary Credit in favour of the exporter. The importer supplies his bank with details of the transaction on an application form. By agreeing to open the credit, the importer's bank guarantees to pay the exporter if the importer cannot or will not pay.

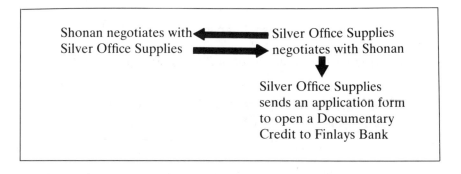

Shonan negotiates with Silver Office Supplies
Silver Office Supplies negotiates with Shonan

Silver Office Supplies sends an application form to open a Documentary Credit to Finlays Bank

Next, the importer's bank (the ISSUING bank) sends details of the Documentary Credit to the exporter's bank (or to its agent bank in the exporter's country). At this stage, the exporter's bank may EITHER simply pass on the details of the Documentary Credit to the exporter, in which case it is an ADVISING bank, OR add its own guarantee to the credit, in which case it is a CONFIRMING bank. If the credit is CONFIRMED, the transaction is very safe for the exporter, because TWO banks have promised to pay him if the importer does not, and if the importer's bank does not pay him, then the CONFIRMING bank will.

## UNIT FIVE

When the exporter receives the Documentary Credit details from his bank he checks them very carefully. These details tell him which documents he must prepare before he can be paid.

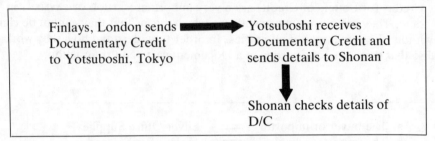

The next stage is for the exporter to prepare the documents which are named in the Documentary Credit, for example,

Bill of Lading (shipping document)
Commercial Invoice
Certificate of Insurance

and then to despatch the goods. The Bill of Lading is signed by the ship's captain to confirm that the goods are on board ship.

After this, the exporter takes the documents to his bank, which checks them. If they are in order
the CONFIRMING bank pays the exporter, or accepts a Bill of Exchange.

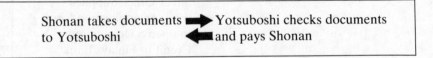

At this point, the exporter has his money, or a Bill of Exchange, the goods are on board ship, and the CONFIRMING bank has the documents.

The CONFIRMING bank then sends the documents to the importer's bank, the ISSUING bank, which checks them and sends the money to the CONFIRMING bank.

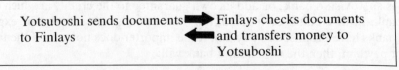

## UNIT FIVE

(If the exporter's bank has not CONFIRMED the Documentary Credit, but only ADVISED him of it, the exporter will not be paid until the ISSUING bank has checked the documents and transferred the money, or accepted a Bill of Exchange.)

The next stage is for the importer's bank to debit the importer's account. The importer must pay his bank in order to get the documents. Without the documents, and in particular without the Bill of Lading, the importer cannot collect the goods.

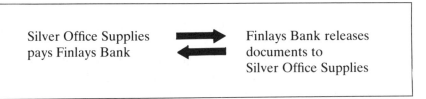

At this point, the importer's bank has been paid, the importer has the documents and the goods are on board ship.

The final stage is for the importer to use the documents, which prove his ownership of the goods, to collect the goods when they arrive in port.

> Silver Office Supplies presents documents and claims goods
>
> when they arrive in Southampton

It is important to realise that banks operate solely on the basis of documents. If the documents are in order, they will pay. The bank is not concerned with whether the goods are satisfactory or not. For their services, banks charge about ¼% of the value of the Documentary Credit.

**Exercise 5.12**
*Check your*
*understanding*

Work in groups.
Study these details of a Confirmed Irrevocable Documentary Credit transaction between Techno Products plc, Manchester, England – the EXPORTER – and Marlin Electronics Inc, Toronto, Canada – the IMPORTER.

These sentences are in the WRONG order. You must put them in the RIGHT order.
Use these words when discussing your answer and writing it down.

## UNIT FIVE

Firstly, Then, At this stage, After this, At this point,
The next stage, Next, Finally.

Marlin presents the documents and claims the goods.
Techno and Marlin agree a sales contract.
The Toronto bank checks the documents and transfers money
to the Manchester bank.
Techno despatches the goods.
Marlin asks its bank in Toronto to open a Documentary
Credit.
Techno checks the Documentary Credit and prepares the
documents.
The Toronto Bank opens a Documentary Credit and sends
the details to the Manchester bank.
The Toronto bank debits Marlin's account and hands over
the documents.
The Manchester bank sends the documents to the Toronto
bank.
Techno presents the documents to the Manchester bank and
is paid.
The Manchester bank sends details of the Documentary
Credit to Techno and confirms the credit.

Begin like this:

*Firstly, Techno and Marlin agree a sales contract. Then,
Marlin asks . . .*

**Exercise 5.13**
*Focus on vocabulary*

Choose one of these words to complete these sentences.
Use the word in its correct form.

catalogue     brochure
leaflet        booklet

a  We need some very impressive _____ for the Frankfurt
    Trade Fair – lots of colour and really glossy paper.
b  A 10-page _____, giving full instructions in English,
    French, Spanish and Italian, is enclosed.
c  The 200-page, fully-illustrated _____ contains full details
    of our complete range of products.
d  Ask the printers if they can get this advertisement onto a
    one-page _____.

cancel      delay
postpone      extend

**e**   Tomorrow's meeting has been _____ until March 21st.

**f**   As you have been unable to meet the agreed delivery date, we have no alternative but to _____ the order.

**g**   We are sorry that your goods arrived late. The _____ was caused by mechanical problems with our new machines.

**h**   We will not be able to meet the deadline for delivery. Ask them if they are willing to _____ it.

**Exercise 5.14**
*Letter writing*

Here is part of a letter from A Clausen, 95 Kongensgade, Kobenhavn, to Azulejos Pedro Baptista, Rua de Alfandega 72–76, 4000 Porto, Portugal.

---

```
We have recently received several large orders from our customers and
would therefore like to increase our order to 8,000 'Coimbra' tiles.
In addition, we would like to place an order for 5,000 'Cintra' floor
tiles.  We enclose our official order form for these goods.
```

---

This is the middle paragraph and is in the correct style. From the six paragraphs below choose the first and last paragraph and write out the whole letter. Only two of the paragraphs are in the correct style.

**a**   We will be eternally grateful if you could arrange the simultaneous shipment of our total order in accordance with the original terms as we agreed on the telephone earlier today. We await your formal confirmation of the above details.

**b**   We've got your confirmation of our order for 5,000 wall tiles. Thanks a lot.

**c**   We'd like you to send all the goods as one lot. Same terms as before as agreed on the phone. Please confirm this.

**d**   We would appreciate it if you would confirm that all the goods are to be despatched together, on the same terms as the original order, as agreed in our telephone conversation this morning.

**e**   It was with the greatest pleasure that we received your prompt confirmation of our order, No 79791, for 5,000 'Coimbra' wall tiles.

**f**   We thank you for your confirmation of our order, No 79791, for 5,000 'Coimbra' wall tiles.

# UNIT FIVE

## The Bank of England

The Bank of England was founded in 1694 by a group of wealthy merchants and landowners for the purpose of raising a loan for King William III in order to finance his war against Louis XIV, King of France. Although it was a private bank, it enjoyed a special relationship with the government, and became, in effect, the government's bank. In 1946 the Bank of England was nationalised and since then has been formally under the control of the Treasury, the government's financial ministry. The Governor of the Bank of England is appointed, in theory, by the Queen, in practice by the Prime Minister on the advice of the Chancellor of the Exchequer.

As the government's bank, the Bank of England carries out many functions. It runs the accounts of government departments and handles the government's vast number of financial payments, receipts and transfers. It also raises money for the government by the sale of government securities and treasury bills. Government securities, or gilts, are long-term fixed interest loans, repayable by the government at a fixed date up to twenty years in the future. Treasury bills are short-term loans sold at a discount and repaid at their face value after ninety-one days. Another responsibility of the bank is the issue of bank notes. It is the only bank in England and Wales which is allowed to issue bank notes, although in Scotland and Northern Ireland the commercial banks issue their own notes. Finally, the Bank of England manages the gold and currency reserves and by buying and selling these can influence the sterling exchange rate.

The Bank of England is also the bankers' bank, since all banks doing sterling business in the United Kingdom are required to have accounts with it. Commercial banks use these accounts to make payments to one another. The Bank of England can influence the behaviour of commercial banks by controlling the amount of money it requires them to deposit in their accounts. If it increases the amount required, then the banks will have less money to lend to their customers, and this will have an effect on the economy as a whole.

The Bank of England exercises general authority and supervision over the banking and financial system in the United Kingdom, maintaining good order and confidence. The Bank is situated in Threadneedle Street, in the heart of the City of London.

**Exercise 5.15**
*Things to find out*

Find out about one of these topics. Report what you have learnt in writing or as a short talk.

**a** The central bank in your own country
**b** Treasury Bills and Government Securities
**c** Exchange rates

# UNIT SIX

**Exercise 6.1** Here is a reply from The New Art Manufacturing Company to an order they have received for sofa-beds. Read it carefully and answer the questions that follow.

The New Art Manufacturing
Company Ltd
96-98 Wood Lane
Chiswick
London
W5A 3EU

Tel: 01 747 2323
Cables: NEWART
Telex: 375232 NAMC G
VAT Registration No 161 4269 64

Registered Office:
96 Wood Lane London W5A 3EU
Registered No: 317889 England

Mr J Schmidt
Chief Buyer
Kurt Schiller Gmb H
Freidensstr. 44
2000 Hamburg 50
West Germany

Your ref: JS/12
Our ref: GD/hd

4 June 19—

Dear Mr Schmidt

Your order (No 1331) for sofa-beds

We thank you for your order for twenty sofa-beds, which we received today.

We are glad to confirm that we can supply the above order from stock, and we enclose a pro-forma invoice for the goods, C I F Hamburg.

The order will be despatched as soon as we have received confirmation of your Documentary Credit from Finlays Bank in London. We have already contacted our forwarding agent to make arrangements for the transportation of the goods, and we assure you that we can meet your delivery deadline of 31 July.

We look forward to hearing of the safe arrival of your order and to doing further business with you.

Yours sincerely

Georgina Dickenson

Georgina Dickenson (Ms)

Enc. Pro-forma invoice

***Check your understanding*** According to the information in the letter, are the following statements TRUE or FALSE or is there NOT ENOUGH INFORMATION to say?

## UNIT SIX

The New Art Manufacturing Company Ltd:

**a** are able to despatch the goods immediately.

**b** enclose a demand for payment before the goods are despatched.

**c** have instructed their freight forwarders to despatch the goods as soon as payment is received.

**d** have an account at Finlays Bank.

**e** will arrange for the insurance of the goods until they reach Hamburg.

Now read the letter again. Close your book and give an oral summary of the letter. Your partner will remind you of anything you miss out.

*Focus on functions:*
*What should you say when*
*you reply to an order?*

**1** Acknowledge receipt of the order.

**2** Confirm that you are able to supply the goods.

**3** Say what you have done about the order.

**4** Say what you are going to do next about the order.

**5** Assure the buyer that you can meet the conditions of the order.

**6** Close the letter.

**A** Match the sentences in Georgina Dickenson's letter with the functions listed above.

**B** Match the sentences below with the list of functions.

**a** We look forward to hearing that your order has arrived safely and to doing business with you in future.

**b** We thank you for your order, No 2222, for cotton shirts, which we received yesterday.

**c** You may be sure that we will carry out your instructions in full.

**d** Thank you for your order of 21st March for . . .

**e** You can depend on us to despatch the goods promptly.

**f** We are glad to confirm that we can supply the above order.

**g** You can rely on us to follow your instructions to the letter.

**h** The goods will be despatched on receipt of . . .

**i** We can confirm that we are able to supply the above order from stock.

**j** Please find enclosed . . .

**k** We will despatch the goods immediately we have received . . .

**l** We have already despatched a pro-forma invoice.

**Exercise 6.2**  Complete this letter. Use the model letter and list of functions on pages 22–23 to help you.

COMPUTERS

1-33 Kitashinjuku 7-Chome Shinjuku-ku Tokyo 160

Tel: 03 342 2244 Telex: 2322403 SHONAN J Cables: SHONCOM

```
Mr D Jackson                        Your ref: DJ/wa
Chief Buyer                         Our ref: AS/tg
Silver Office Supplies
14 North Street
London EC1 7AD
United Kingdom                      2 March 19-
```

Dear Mr Jackson

We thank you _____(1) your order, No YT954, _____(2) 600 SCROLL word processors, _____(3) we received today.  We are glad to hear that you were so impressed _____(4) the demonstration given _____(5) Mr Nixon.

We are pleased to be able _____(6) confirm that we _____(7) supply the order from stock, and we _____(8) a pro-forma invoice _____(9) the goods, CIF Southampton.

The goods will be despatched when our bank _____(10) the Documentary Credit.  You may rely _____(11) us to carry _____(12) the instructions in the Documentary Credit in _____(13), and we can assure you that the goods will be delivered _____(14) 30 March.

We look forward to hearing of the safe _____(15) of your order and to _____(16) further orders from you soon.

Yours _____(17)

A Suzuki
Sales Manager


Enc. _____(18)

# UNIT SIX

**Exercise 6.3**
*Focus on punctuation:*
*The comma – part three*

WHAT IS THE DIFFERENCE IN MEANING BETWEEN THE FOLLOWING TWO SENTENCES?

**a**  The goods, which were packed in wooden crates, were despatched from Copenhagen on 1st April.

**b**  The goods which were packed in wooden crates were despatched from Copenhagen on 1st April.

In the first sentence, the words 'which were packed in wooden crates' are separated from the rest of the sentence by commas. It is extra information about the goods.
In the second sentence the words 'which were packed in wooden crates' are not separated from the rest of the sentence by commas. This is because they identify the goods by the way they are packed, distinguishing them from other orders packed differently and despatched from different places.

Now punctuate these sentences in the way which is most likely according to the situation.

**a**  mr nixon who represents our company in london will visit head office on 12th july

**b**  all the items which were packed in wooden boxes arrived safely whereas several of the items which were packed in cardboard boxes arrived damaged

**c**  mrs bush who joined the company forty years ago is retiring on friday

**d**  the disk which contained the information you require was accidentally destroyed

**e**  the man who got the job had better qualifications than the other candidates

**f**  mr frayn who got the job had better qualifications than the other candidates

**Exercise 6.4**
*Listen to this:*
*Dictation practice*

Mrs Margaret Corbett, Sales Manager of Techno Products plc, 30 Thorpe Way, Manchester, has received an order letter and left her reply on cassette for you to write. Write down your company's name and address, then listen to the cassette and write the letter.

**Exercise 6.5**
*Letter writing*

Mr George Armstrong, Sales Manager of Shiptons Cross Country Vehicles, has handed you the order letter from Across Africa Safaris Ltd, with his notes written on it. He has asked you to prepare a reply for his signature.

..... for the catalogues and price lists which you sent us on 10 April.

We have also met your representative and had the opportunity to drive the Ranger vehicle. We are convinced that your vehicles will be suitable for our needs. We discussed terms of payment with Mr Munro and he offered us a 10% discount on the C I F Mombasa price. *O.k.* He also assured us that the vehicles could be painted in our company's colours, black and green, at no extra charge. *Yes, we can do this*

We are therefore placing an order for eight Ranger vehicles and enclose our official order form, No 987, for these vehicles.

*make sure it is Irrevocable*
We would like to confirm that, as discussed with Mr Munro, payment is to be made by Documentary Credit. We are therefore instructing Finlays Bank International, Nairobi, to open a Documentary Credit in your favour, C I F Mombassa. *O.k.*

*No problem*
Please note that delivery before 14 August is essential as ...

**Exercise 6.6**
*How to say it*

You often see these abbreviations in business documents. You say them as separate letters.
Work with a partner.
Ask what the abbreviations stand for. Your partner should look at the inside back cover of the book for the answers.

AGM
IOU
AOB
PA
VIP
PTO

## UNIT SIX

**Exercise 6.7**
*How to say it*

You can find these abbreviations in memos, informal notes and advertisements, and on envelopes.

If you have to read aloud a document with these abbreviations in, you say the full form in words, not the letters of the abbreviation.

| | |
|---|---|
| ono | or nearest offer |
| asap | as soon as possible |
| tba | to be arranged |
| pt | part time |
| pw | per week |
| pcm | per calendar month |
| pa | per annum |
| c/o | care of |
| vgc | very good condition |
| wef | with effect from |
| cc | copies to |
| aae | according to age and experience |

These Latin abbreviations are used in English and are read aloud either as separate letters or in their full English form:

| | |
|---|---|
| ie | that is |
| eg | for example |
| nb | note (well) that |

These should always be read aloud in their English form:

| | |
|---|---|
| viz | namely |
| cf | compare |

nb also:

| | |
|---|---|
| etc | et cetera OR and so on |
| re | about, concerning, said as 'ray' |

When using the 24-hour clock, we say 1500 hours as 'fifteen hundred hours'.

Work with a partner.
Identify the following extracts. What are they? Where do they come from? Read them out loud.

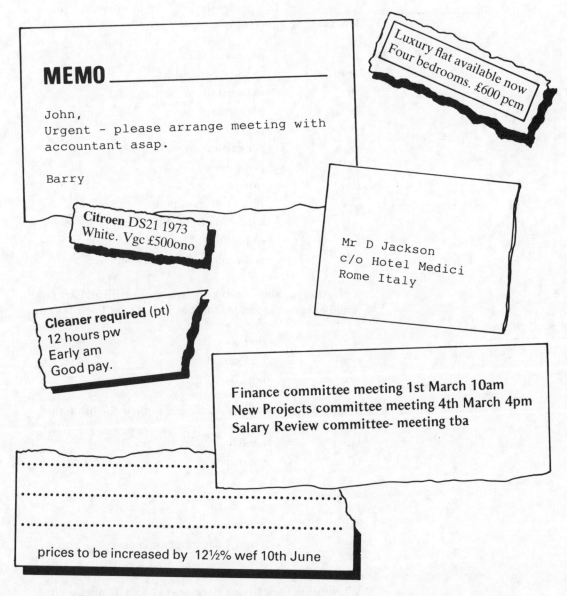

**MEMO** _____

John,
Urgent - please arrange meeting with accountant asap.

Barry

Luxury flat available now
Four bedrooms. £600 pcm

**Citroen** DS21 1973
White. Vgc £500ono

Mr D Jackson
c/o Hotel Medici
Rome Italy

**Cleaner required** (pt)
12 hours pw
Early am
Good pay.

**Finance committee meeting 1st March 10am**
**New Projects committee meeting 4th March 4pm**
**Salary Review committee- meeting tba**

prices to be increased by 12½% wef 10th June

**Exercise 6.8**
*Listen to this*

Bill Patterson, Manager of The Old Country Clothing Company, 1195–1200 North Lakeside Drive, Montreal, Quebec, Canada, is a regular customer of West Highland Tweed Mills Ltd, Portree, Isle of Skye, Scotland. He is telephoning Angus MacDonald, the Manager of the Scottish company, to place an order for tweed.

Listen to their conversation and fill in the order checklist, which Angus MacDonald completes as he listens to the order, with the required information.

---

# West Highland Tweed Mills Ltd

Order Form for Telephone Orders only

Customer Details:

   NAME OF COMPANY: The Old Country Clothing Company

   PERSON TO CONTACT: Bill Patterson

   ADDRESS: 1195-1200 North Lakeside Drive,
   Montreal, Canada

Order Details:

| | Quantity required | Pattern | Colours |
|---|---|---|---|
| 1 | 300 rolls | Herringbone | ............... |
| 2 | ............... | Herringbone | ............... |
| 3 | ............... | Dog's tooth check | ............... |
| 4 | ............... | Dog's tooth check | ............... |
| 5 | ............... | Plain | ............... |

Delivery Date: ............................................

Method of Payment: .......................................

Action Required: .........................................

Accepted by: .............................................

---

**Exercise 6.9**
*Letter writing*    Write a letter from West Highland Tweed Mills Ltd to The Old Country Clothing Company. Formally accept the order and enclose a pro-forma invoice. Lay out the letter correctly and use the model letter and list of functions on pages 74–75 to help you plan the contents. Take the information you need from the completed telephone order form.

# UNIT SIX

**Exercise 6.10**
*Letter writing*

The following letter was typed to dictation by a trainee who was told to lay it out correctly, ready for Mr Jackson's signature. However, when Mr Jackson was about to sign, he noticed that it was full of mistakes. He has passed the letter to you for correction.

Re-write the letter, correcting all the mistakes.

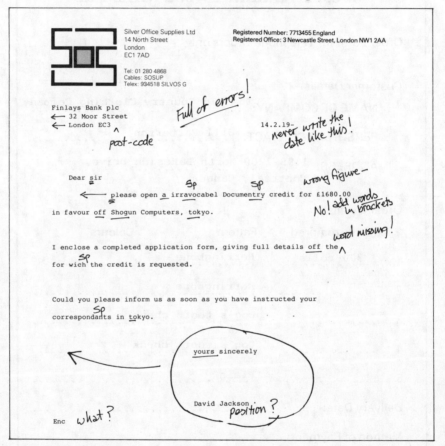

**Exercise 6.11**
*Check your understanding of the application form to open a Documentary Credit*

Here is the completed application form to open a documentary credit that Silver Office Supplies sent to their bank. Study the details and answer these questions. The bold numbers show you where to look for the answers.

a   Which word tells you that this documentary credit cannot be changed or cancelled without the agreement of all parties? **2**
b   Who will pay and who will be paid? **1** and **3**
c   Give the names of the importer's bank and the exporter's bank. **4, 5**
d   How will the exporter's bank be informed of the details of the documentary credit? **5**

**e** Who will inform Shonan which documents they will have to produce? **5**

**f** When will Shonan receive payment? **6**

**g** Which documents must Shonan present to their bank? **7**

**h** Who has insured the goods? **8**

**i** Will Shonan still be paid if neither Silver Office Supplies nor Finlays Bank are willing to pay? **9**

| | |
|---|---|
| **1** SENDER    Silver Office Supplies<br>14 North Street<br>London EC1 7AD | **INSTRUCTIONS TO OPEN<br>A DOCUMENTARY CREDIT** |

| | | |
|---|---|---|
| **2** PLEASE OPEN THE FOLLOWING:<br>☑ IRREVOCABLE<br>☐ REVOCABLE DOCUMENTARY CREDIT | PLACE:   London<br>DATE:<br>14th February 19- | BENEFICIARY'S BANK<br>(IF KNOWN)<br><br>The Yotsuboshi<br>Bank |
| **3** BENEFICIARY   Shonan Computers k.k.<br>1-33 Kitashinjuku 7-chome<br>Shinjuku-ku Tokyo 160 | Finlays Bank<br>32 Moor Street<br>London EC2 | 64-28 Otemachi<br>5-chome<br>Chiyoda-ku Tokyo |
| AMOUNT:   £168 000 | **4** | **5** |

| | |
|---|---|
| DATE AND PLACE<br>OF EXPIRY    18th May London | PLEASE ADVISE THIS BANK:<br>☐ BY LETTER     ☑ BY TELEX<br>☐ BY CABLE |
| PARTIAL SHIPMENT<br>☐ ALLOWED     ☑ NOT ALLOWED | TRANSHIPMENT<br>☐ ALLOWED     ☑ NOT ALLOWED |
| TERMS OF SHIPMENT (FOB, CIF, C&F)<br>CIF Southampton | **8** GOODS INSURED BY ☐ US ☑ SELLER |

| | | |
|---|---|---|
| DESPATCH FROM<br>Yokohama | FOR TRANSPORTATION TO<br>Southampton | LATEST DATE OF SHIPMENT<br>10th April 19- |

DOCUMENTS MUST BE PRESENTED NOT LATER THAN   21   DAYS AFTER DATE OF DESPATCH

**6** BENEFICIARY MAY DISPOSE OF THE CREDIT AMOUNT AS FOLLOWS:
☑ AT SIGHT UPON PRESENTATION OF DOCUMENTS
☐ AFTER...DAYS CALCULATED FROM DATE OF....
☐ BY A DRAFT DUE ON....DRAWN ON ☐ YOU ☐ YOUR CORRESPONDENTS
    WHICH YOU/YOUR CORRESPONDENTS WILL PLEASE ACCEPT

**7** AGAINST SURRENDER OF THE FOLLOWING DOCUMENTS:

| | |
|---|---|
| ☑ INVOICE (3 COPIES)<br>    SHIPPING DOCUMENT<br>☑ SEA: BILL OF LADING<br>☐ RAIL: DUPLICATE WAYBILL | ☐ AIR: AIR WAYBILL<br>☑ INSURANCE CERTIFICATE (3 COPIES)<br>    COVERING THE FOLLOWING RISKS<br>☐ ADDITIONAL DOCUMENTS (SPECIFY) |

| | |
|---|---|
| NOTIFY ADDRESS   Silver Office Supplies Ltd<br>IN BILL OF LADING   14 North Street   London   EC1 7AD | GOODS   600 Scroll 2000<br>word processors |

**9** YOUR CORRESPONDENTS TO ADVISE BENEFICIARY
☑ ADDING THEIR CONFIRMATION      ☐ NOT ADDING THEIR CONFIRMATION

| | |
|---|---|
| PAYMENT TO BE DEBITED TO OUR<br>Sterling ACCOUNT NO. 3850061 | SIGNATURE:   P Jackson |

# UNIT SIX

**Exercise 6.12**
*Prepositions of time*

Notice this sentence from the order letter in Unit Four:

'Delivery by 30th March essential.'

Must the order be delivered on 30th March?

Read the following list of orders and pay special attention to the words which tell you when things should be done.

Silver Office Supplies Ltd
14 North Street
London
EC1 7AD

Registered Number: 7713455 England
Registered Office: 3 Newcastle Street, London NW1 2AA

Tel: 01 280 4868
Cables: SOSUP
Telex: 934518 SILVOS G

ORDERS RECEIVED ON:    20th March

| ORDER NUMBER | CUSTOMER | COMMENTS |
|---|---|---|
| 1126/EP | Exco plc | Deliver on 28th. N.B. not before or after |
| 32525/BT | Brian Taylor Associates | Deliver by 31st. Goods ready now.    Despatch tomorrow. |
| 975/HM | H P Morris & Sons | Deliver between 9 and 12 noon Mon-Fri. |
| 44956/TR | Trends Ltd | Deliver within 14 days, ie, not later than 4th April. |
| 77922/ITC | Ipswich Trading Company | Deliver immediately. Original order received seven days ago.    Lost? |
| RG/1925 | Robert Greene and Partners | Not in stock yet.    Customer prepared to wait for seven days only, ie until 27 March. |
| JS/4452 | John Smith (Chelsea) Ltd | N.B. special order.    John Smith has been a customer since 1970.    Deliver before 5 pm today. |

# UNIT SIX

Are the following statements TRUE or FALSE according to the information in the order list?

**a**  Exco will accept goods up to 28th March.
**b**  Brian Taylor will accept delivery only on 31st March.
**c**  Robert Greene will accept delivery on 27th March.
**d**  H P Morris will accept delivery at 11 o'clock on Tuesday.
**e**  John Smith has been a customer for more than twenty years.
**f**  The Ipswich Trading Company's original order was received after 13th March.

**Exercise 6.13**
*Oral practice:*
*Giving information*

Work with a partner.
Student A has a list of order numbers and delivery dates and reads the information to Student B. Student B should write down the information and read it back to Student A.

For example:

Student A says:

| ORDER NUMBER | COMMENTS |
|---|---|
| PQ/5922 | not later than 15th July |

Student B writes and then says:
Deliver order number PQ/5922 by 15th July.

---

TODAY'S DATE:     10th July 19–

| ORDER NUMBER: | COMMENTS |
|---|---|
| TG/6753 | not later than 17th July |
| 3131K | 18th July only |
| 77525/LM | 19th – 24th July |
| 2665/ZX | 14 days from today (or earlier) |
| 9434/TG | first ordered 4th July – not received by customer |
| 5222/FA | not received – customer expected delivery 7th July |
| 6271/OP | not later than 14 days after the last day of July |

---

**Exercise 6.14**
*Focus on vocabulary*

The words 'stock' and 'store' can be used in several ways. Read these sentences and match them with the meanings in the list below.

**a**  We don't stock those goods.
**b**  We don't have those goods in stock.
**c**  There is nowhere to store these goods.
**d**  He used £5,000 of his savings to buy government stock.
**e**  We can deliver from stock.
**f**  We are stockists of all major brands.
**g**  The shop will close at 4 pm today for stocktaking.
**h**  Dickens and Swans provides in-store foreign exchange facilities.
**i**  During hot weather meat is kept in the cold store.

1  a refrigerated room
2  temporary unavailability of goods
3  services provided on the premises
4  never supplying particular goods
5  checking the quantity of goods
6  regular suppliers of goods
7  lack of space
8  an investment of money
9  immediately available goods

## Banking

In the City of London you can see literally dozens of banks, both British and foreign, in every street. There are the headquarters, and several branches, of the major British banks, Barclays, Lloyds, Midland and National Westminster – which occupies the tallest building in London. These banks have a branch network all over the United Kingdom and provide 'retail' banking services for individuals as well as for both large and small companies. They offer two kinds of accounts – deposit accounts which bear interest and current accounts for which a cheque book is provided to withdraw and transfer money. The clearing of cheques, together with other money transfer systems, is a major activity of these banks, which is why they are called 'clearing banks'. They co-operate to clear cheques through the Bankers' Clearing House, a centralised cheque-clearing system based in the City of London.

Unlike the clearing banks, merchant banks do not normally provide services to the general public. They are specialised 'wholesale' banks, with a small staff and no branch network, which raise loans for large companies and governments, and provide financial and investment advice. They are involved in the financing of international trade, and will accept, or guarantee, Bills of Exchange, which is why they are sometimes referred to as 'accepting houses'.

Foreign banks in London generally concentrate on international banking, particularly in the Eurodollar market – Eurodollars are US dollars held in bank accounts outside the USA.

However, recently some foreign banks have begun to lend money to companies in Britain, and a few have started to offer banking services to the general public, although on a limited scale, since they do not have a branch network.

Banks are gradually becoming more like one another and it is more accurate to talk of merchant banking and retail banking rather than merchant banks and retail banks. The British clearing banks now have their own merchant banking divisions and are engaged in extensive international operations, and some merchant banks are now offering banking services to the general public. The rapid advances in technology make a branch network less important than it used to be as a basis for offering services to the public. The present trend is for all banks to offer a wide range of financial services to all types of customers.

|                          |                                                                 |
| ------------------------ | --------------------------------------------------------------- |
| **Exercise 6.15**        | Find out about one of these topics. Report what you have        |
| *Things to find out*     | learned in writing or as a short talk.                          |

    **a**   The work of a bank in your own country
    **b**   The clearing of cheques
    **c**   Merchant Banking
    **d**   The Eurodollar market
    **e**   New technology in Banking

# U N I T   S E V E N

**Exercise 7.1**    This telex message gives the same information as a letter you have already read. Which one?

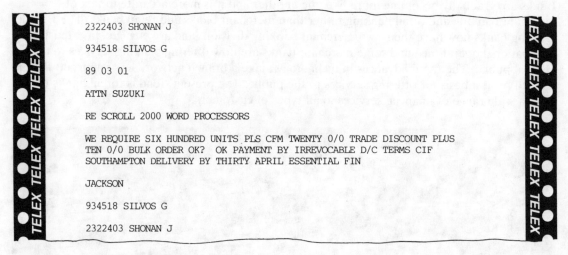

```
2322403 SHONAN J

934518 SILVOS G

89 03 01

ATTN SUZUKI

RE SCROLL 2000 WORD PROCESSORS

WE REQUIRE SIX HUNDRED UNITS PLS CFM TWENTY 0/0 TRADE DISCOUNT PLUS
TEN 0/0 BULK ORDER OK?  OK PAYMENT BY IRREVOCABLE D/C TERMS CIF
SOUTHAMPTON DELIVERY BY THIRTY APRIL ESSENTIAL FIN

JACKSON

934518 SILVOS G

2322403 SHONAN J
```

*Check your understanding*    See the inside back cover of the book for list of abbreviations.

   **a**   What does ATTN mean?
   **b**   What does RE mean?
   **c**   When was the telex sent?

**Exercise 7.2**    Read this telex message quickly and then answer the questions below. You don't have to understand every word.

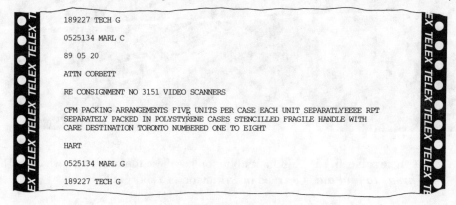

```
189227 TECH G

0525134 MARL C

89 05 20

ATTN CORBETT

RE CONSIGNMENT NO 3151 VIDEO SCANNERS

CFM PACKING ARRANGEMENTS FIVE UNITS PER CASE EACH UNIT SEPARATLYEEEE RPT
SEPARATELY PACKED IN POLYSTYRENE CASES STENCILLED FRAGILE HANDLE WITH
CARE DESTINATION TORONTO NUMBERED ONE TO EIGHT

HART

0525134 MARL G

189227 TECH G
```

   **a**   Who is the message from?
   **b**   Who is it to?
   **c**   What is it about?
   **d**   Does it contain any errors?
   **e**   How must the video scanners be packed?
   **f**   What will you read on the outside of the crates?

# UNIT SEVEN

## Telex: what it is and how it works

*Note taking*   List the points that justify the claim that 'Telex can completely replace ordinary postal deliveries'.

## Worldwide communications

Telex has been around for a long time, in fact half a century and yet it still holds its own very unique position in today's modern communication spectrum. There are few other services that have the same worldwide penetration reaching all parts of the world whether it be in the main technological countries or the developing countries of the third world. In business-to-business communication, get the message across with telex.

International telex puts you in touch with 1.5 million contacts throughout the world. The International service is now available to 200 countries and 190 of these countries can be reached automatically from your telex machine. The telex service also offers satellite and radio links with ships at sea.

## Fast -efficient -flexible

Telex is very flexible; you can use it to make and confirm hotel and travel or other types of reservations – acknowledge orders and confirm delivery schedules – issue quotations and chase payments. As opposed to correspondence that may miss the post, the telex service offers fast written communication with any part of the world, you simply type it here and telex types it there. In fact telex can completely replace ordinary postal deliveries with the speed, reliability and efficiency of modern electronics.

## No time or language problems

You can send a telex at any time of the day or night without anyone needing to be there to answer since their machine will automatically accept, print and acknowledge your message. It will arrive on your customer's desk ready for the immediate response a telex message demands. With telex there is no risk of being overheard and there is no danger of misunderstanding or language difficulties.

## Modern machines -simple to use

The modern telex terminals that are now available will blend into any office environment not just because of their attractive design or ease of use but also because of their extremely low operating noise. Today's modern machines allow anyone who can use a typewriter or computer keyboard to feel immediately at home using telex. For those of us who are two finger typists, easy editing is available so that when the message is transmitted it is both word perfect and forwarded at maximum speed saving on transmission costs.

## Economic worldwide communications

In addition to its speed, international timing, flexibility and inherent status, telex is also an extremely cost effective way of sending any written message for either commercial purposes or person to person executive communication. Telexes are concise and to the point and therefore both economic and forceful.

## Got the message?

All telex subscribers in the world have their own unique answerback code, so as soon as their machine receives a message the answerback confirms that your telex has reached its destination.

To gain the maximum benefit from a service that is used worldwide you need to display your full telex answerback prominently and correctly on all your stationery – demonstrate your company's efficiency – show you mean business.

## More power at your finger tips -Telex Plus

Designed to complement the capabilities of your telex terminal, the facility Telex Plus* is available to anyone who has a telex machine. It will deal with single or multi-address telexes, making repeat attempts when necessary and automatically confirming delivery. There is nothing to buy, no membership or subscription fee, just use Telex Plus as and when you need it.

## Demonstrates your company's professionalism

If you thought that the only way to originate a telex message was to own a telex machine you would be wrong. Within today's diverse technology there are many ways open to you; for example by using your word processor with a telex interface. Whichever way it's done, however, using telex immediately identifies your company as a progressive and efficient organisation. It is backed up by all the advanced technology and investment of British Telecom International who continue to set standards of service that lead the world.

## International Telex -how can you manage without it?

If you would like further details of how International Telex can help the efficiency of your business, contact Arthur Langstone by telex 21601 BTI G or telephone 01-936-2756

Due to BTI's policy of continual improvement, services and facilities may be modified, added to, or withdrawn.

*Telex Plus is a Trade Mark of British Telecommunications plc

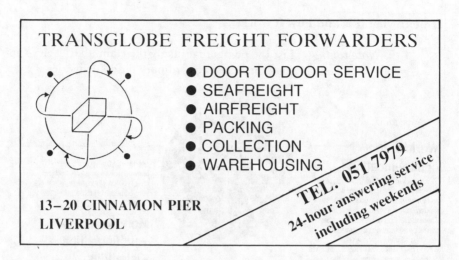

TRANSGLOBE FREIGHT FORWARDERS

● DOOR TO DOOR SERVICE
● SEAFREIGHT
● AIRFREIGHT
● PACKING
● COLLECTION
● WAREHOUSING

13–20 CINNAMON PIER
LIVERPOOL

TEL. 051 7979
24-hour answering service
including weekends

**Exercise 7.3**
*Finding information in advertisements*

Having received the telex from Marlin Electronics giving packing instructions, Mrs Corbett has asked you to look in Yellow Pages and find companies which can make the necessary transport arrangements.

Look at the advertisements above and on page 91 and identify the company that:

**a** provides a service for a specific industry
**b** specialises in carrying goods to a particular part of the world
**c** provides a service for private individuals as well as businesses
**d** can be contacted at any time

**Exercise 7.4**

John,

I need some information about timetables and freight rates in connection with our export order for video scanners to Toronto. These companies look the most suitable, but I need more information. Would you do a letter of enquiry for me to sign?

Margaret.

**Exercise 7.5**
*How to say it*

In catalogues, brochures, price lists and specifications you often see abbreviations for weights and measurements. Make sure you know how to say them.

| | |
|---|---|
| cat. no. M/032 | catalogue number em stroke oh three two |
| 100 cm$^3$ | one hundred cubic centimetres |
| 30 cm$^2$ | thirty square centimetres |
| 5 m × 4 m | five metres by four metres |
| 6′ × 3′ × 2′ | six feet by three feet by two feet |
| 10″ × 8″ | ten inches by eight inches |
| $\frac{2}{3}$ | two-thirds |
| $\frac{1}{4}$ | a quarter |
| 5$\frac{3}{16}$ | five and three sixteenths |
| 10 lb 8 oz | ten pounds eight ounces |

Work with a partner.
Say these sentences aloud. Your partner should write them down.

**a**  The cat. no. is P/041
**b**  The capacity of the container is 200 cm$^3$
**c**  The area of the room is 16 m$^2$
**d**  The exact measurement is 3 $\frac{5}{16}$″
**e**  The crate measures 10′ × 3′ × 2′
**f**  This parcel weighs 4 lb 15 oz – nearly 5 lb

**Exercise 7.6**
*Check your understanding*

One of the freight forwarders that Mrs Corbett wrote to sent her a booklet containing information about the different forms of transport available for exporting goods. Study this extract from it and answer the questions that follow.

**The Transglobe Guide for New Exporters**

|  | *Advantages* | *Disadvantages* | *Suitable Cargoes* |
|---|---|---|---|
| **Road** | inexpensive, door-to-door service | traffic jams, accidents, delays at frontiers | almost all goods except heavy bulky goods |
| **Rail** | safe fast | expensive, station to station only | very heavy goods, eg coal, iron ore |
| **Air** | fast safe | very expensive, goods must be collected from and delivered to airport | light, high value goods, perishable goods |
| **Sea** | covers long distances, inexpensive | not fast, goods must be taken to and from docks | almost everything, charged by volume |

What do you think would be the most suitable means of transport for the following goods?

a   10 one-kilogram gold bars from Hong Kong to Japan.
b   200 industrial diamonds from Amsterdam to Sheffield.
c   1,000 tonnes of timber from Stockholm to Dublin.
d   300 kilograms of ceramic tiles from Lisbon to Copenhagen.
e   200 dozen flowers from Jersey to London.
f   500 tonnes of iron ore from Australia to Japan.
g   100 kilograms of mangoes from Calcutta to Paris.
h   2 racehorses from London to Paris.
i   10 designer dresses from Milan to Frankfurt.
j   1,000 tonnes of coal from Poland to Austria.

# UNIT SEVEN

**Exercise 7.7**
*Writing a*
*short report*

Work in groups of three or four.

Mrs Corbett has asked you to advise her on the despatch arrangements for three orders. Look at the details of the consignments and the information and timetables you have obtained.

Choose how best to send the goods. Write a short report to Mrs Corbett.

## CONSIGNMENTS

11th JUNE 19--

| PRODUCT | QUANTITY | UNIT PRICE | WEIGHT PER UNIT | DIMENSIONS PER UNIT | DESTINATION | REMARKS |
|---|---|---|---|---|---|---|
| Satellite Dishes | 10 | £5000 | 500kg | 2x2x2m | Melbourne | Already three weeks overdue! Penalty clause – 1% reduction in price for every week overdue! |
| Electronic Programmers | 100 | £10 | 500gm | 10x8x4cm | Istanbul | Must be delivered by 17th June! |
| Air Conditioning Units | 20 | £200 | 10 Kilos | 100x50x30cm | Iquitos | |

**TRANSGLOBE**

Transglobe Freight Forwarders
13-20 Cinnamon Pier
Liverpool LP8 2YD

Tel: 051 797 7041
Cables: TRANSFOR
Telex: 875671 TRANSGLO G

Registered office: 1 Peel Street Liverpool LP3 2PS
Registered in England: No 174692

..................................................................
..................................................................
............ daily flights to all European destinations. We confirm that we are able to find space on cargo flights to Australia, which leave twice a week on Wednesday and Sunday. The rate for all these flights is £3 per kilogram. With regard to your enquiry about flights to Peru, we are sorry to inform you that there are no direct flights from Manchester, but there are regular flights from Heathrow, London to Lima. The goods are then transported by local air services to Iquitos ............. .

.............. the cheapest way of transporting goods to Turkey is by road. Container lorries depart daily from our Manchester depot. The journey takes 5 - 7 days ........................................
..................................................................

93

# The Seven Seas Shipping Company

```
SAILINGS FROM LIVERPOOL

DEPARTS          DESTINATION          ARRIVES

15th June        Wellington           9th July

18th June        Melbourne            9th July

19th June        Jakarta              6th July

19th June        Buenos Aires         29th June

22nd June        Iquitos              2nd July

23rd July        Rio de Janeiro       3rd July


NOTE:  Freight rates £100 per cubic metre for all these voyages
```

**Exercise 7.8**
*Focus on vocabulary*

Match the words with the pictures. Write down the number of the picture and the correct letter.

A cardboard box
B crate
C packing case
D carton
E barrel
F bale
G drum
H hessian sack
I carboy
J parcel
K padded envelope (jiffy bag)
L fork-lift truck
M crane
N hook
O chain
P pallet
Q polystyrene mould
R padding
S waterproof lining
T metal bands
U rope
V staples
W nails
X screws
Y glue
Z tape

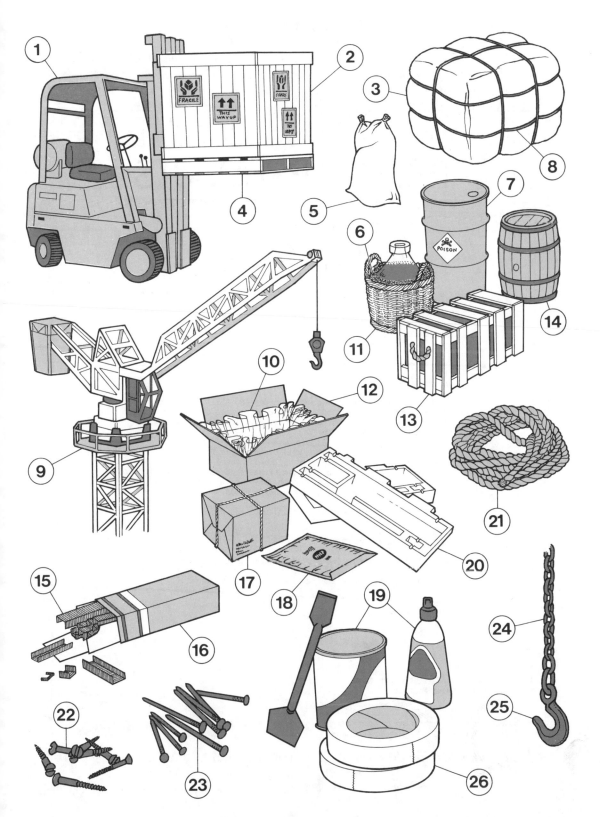

**Exercise 7.9**
*Letter containing packing instructions*
On receiving the telex message from Marlin Electronics, Mrs Corbett wrote this letter to The Seven Seas Shipping Company.

---

# TECHNO PRODUCTS

Techno Products plc
30 Thorpe Way  Manchester MN1 3RT

Tel: 061 660 891 Cables: TECHPRO
Telex: 189227 TECH G Fax (group 3): 061 54541

A Company Registered in England: No 9916670
Registered Office: 2 Seacoal Lane, Manchester MN5 6CB

Mr D Simpson                                          Our ref: MC/WE
Customer Service Manager
The Seven Seas Shipping Company Ltd
20-25 Paddington Quay
Liverpool L15 9YH                                     25 May 19—

Dear Mr Simpson

I am writing to you about our export order (No 3151) for video
scanners, which we discussed last Monday.  We have since received a
telex from Marlin Electronics, Toronto, detailing their packing
instructions for these goods.

As arranged, the video scanners will be available for collection from
our warehouse on 3 June. Each unit has been encased in polystyrene
to protect it from rough handling in transit and packed in a cardboard
box.  Please pack the boxes in wooden cases, five boxes per case.  The
cases must have fireproof and waterproof linings.

The following words should be stencilled on all sides of the cases:

EXPORT - TORONTO
FRAGILE - HANDLE WITH CARE

and the cases should be individually numbered from 1 to 8.

Please ensure that these instructions are followed carefully.

Yours sincerely

*Margaret Corbett*

Margaret Corbett (Mrs)
Sales Manager

---

***Check your understanding***

**a**  Will the Freight Forwarder do all the packing?

**b**  What will happen on June 3rd?

**c**  Why do Marlin want every side of the crates stencilled?

## UNIT SEVEN

**_Focus on functions:_**
**_How do you give packing_**
**_instructions?_**

Find the sentences in the letter that carry out these functions.

State reason for writing.
_I am writing to you in connection with the packing of . . ._
_I am writing to confirm that the units will be packed in . . ._
_I am writing to you with regard to our order . . ._

Give instructions.
_Each unit must be encased in foam rubber and . . ._
_The boxes must be bound with leather straps._
_The crates should have waterproof linings_
_The barrels should be wrapped in hessian._
_Please ensure that the following words are stencilled on . . ._

**Exercise 7.10**
**_Oral practice:_**
**_Passives_**

An inspector from an insurance company is visiting your factory. He wants to know how your goods are packed. If they are packed well, there will be fewer breakages and less damage, and the insurance company will receive fewer claims.

Work with a partner.
Look at the pictures below and on page 98 and continue the following conversation.

INSPECTOR: I'd like to know how your last consignment of video scanners was packed.
DESPATCH CLERK: First of all, they were wrapped in polythene.
INSPECTOR: I see, and then . . .

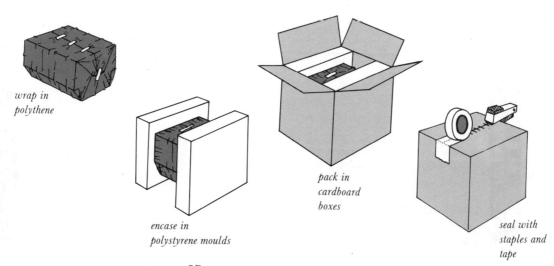

_wrap in
polythene_

_encase in
polystyrene moulds_

_pack in
cardboard
boxes_

_seal with
staples and
tape_

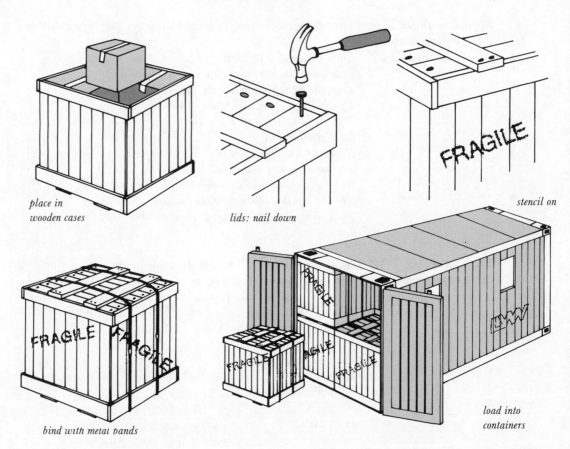

place in
wooden cases

lids: nail down

stencil on

bind with metal bands

load into
containers

**Exercise 7.11**
*Letter writing*

Read this telex and then write a letter for Bill Patterson to sign and send directly to Angus MacDonald to confirm the information in his telex message.

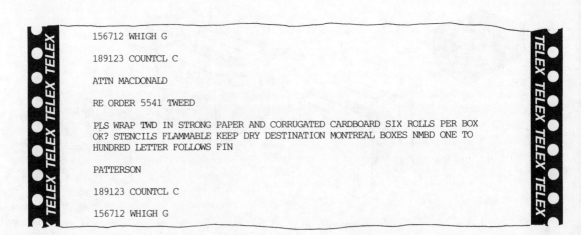

```
156712 WHIGH G

189123 COUNTCL C

ATTN MACDONALD

RE ORDER 5541 TWEED

PLS WRAP TWD IN STRONG PAPER AND CORRUGATED CARDBOARD SIX ROLLS PER BOX
OK? STENCILS FLAMMABLE KEEP DRY DESTINATION MONTREAL BOXES NMBD ONE TO
HUNDRED LETTER FOLLOWS FIN

PATTERSON

189123 COUNTCL C

156712 WHIGH G
```

**Exercise 7.12**
*Letter writing*

The New Art Manufacturing Company have received this telex from one of their customers. Ms Dickenson has asked you to write a letter to the freight forwarder about the packing instructions.

```
375232 NAMC G

5216678 KSCH D

ATTN DICKENSON

RE ORDER NO 1331 TWENTY SOFABEDS

PLS PACK IN SPRT WDN CASES SOFABEDS FIRMLY SECURED TO FLOOR OF CASE
WRAPPED IN CLOSE FITTING POLYTHENE WITH PLASTIC FOAM PADDING CASES
STENCILLED THIS WAY UP INFLAMMABLE DESTINATION HAMBURG CASES NMBD ONE
TO TWENTY

SCHIMDT
5216678 KSCH D

375232 NAMC G
```

 **Exercise 7.13**
*Listen to this*

Listen to the conversation between Mrs Corbett, of Techno Products plc, and Mr Simpson, of The Seven Seas Shipping Company. Mr Simpson is responsible for arranging the packing and transportation of Techno's export consignments. Look at the Bill of Lading on page 100. Make a list of the information which must be added to the B/L. The numbers show you where information is missing.

**Bills of Lading**

A Bill of Lading is a receipt given by the shipping company to say that the goods have been loaded on board ship. It is a document of title, that is, it proves ownership of the goods. The buyer will need a B/L to collect the goods when they arrive at their destination. If a B/L is described as 'clean' it means that the goods were shipped on board in perfect condition. If the captain of the ship notices damage to the packaging or the goods, he will write on the B/L to this effect, and such a B/L is described as 'claused' or 'dirty'.

# The Seven Seas Shipping Company

## 20-25 PADDINGTON QUAY LIVERPOOL L15 9YH

| SHIPPER | VESSEL | B/L No. |
| --- | --- | --- |
| **1** | **2** | REF No.<br><br>**10** |

| CONSIGNEE | PORT OF LOADING |
| --- | --- |
| To order | **3** |
| | PORT OF DESTINATION |
| | **4** |

| NOTIFY ADDRESS | FREIGHT PAYABLE AT |
| --- | --- |
| **5** | Liverpool |

| MARKS & NOS | DESCRIPTION OF GOODS |
| --- | --- |
| **6** | **7** |
| | GROSS WEIGHT |
| | **8** |
| MEASUREMENT IN M³ | |
| **9** | |

| PLACE AND DATE OF ISSUE | SIGNED |
| --- | --- |
| | |

**Exercise 7.14**
*Focus on punctuation:*
*The apostrophe – part one*

Notice how apostrophes are used in these sentences:

**a** Miss Richardson's car was damaged in an accident.
**b** The Health and Safety Inspector's report was critical of our procedures.
**c** Mr Wells's appointment had to be cancelled.
**d** Mr Jackson's secretary's diary has been lost.

## UNIT SEVEN

Now use these words to make complete, correctly-punctuated sentences.

**e**  financial controller/investigation/complete
**f**  mr wilkins/visit/postpone
**g**  christopher/analysis/export orders/useful
**h**  director/chauffeur/uniform/very smart

Notice how apostrophes are used in this sentence:

**i**  We stock a wide range of boys' and men's shirts.

Now use these words to make complete, correctly-punctuated sentences.

**j**  enclose/price list/range/girls/women/fashions
**k**  stockists/all major brands/children/shoes

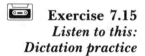 **Exercise 7.15**
*Listen to this:*
*Dictation practice*

Mr Suzuki, of Shonan Computers, has left a letter on cassette for you to write. It informs Silver Office Supplies that their consignment of SCROLL 2000 word processors has been despatched.

Write down the name and address of your company and then listen to the cassette.

## The Baltic Exchange

The Baltic Exchange, situated in the City of London, is an international shipping exchange where traders who have cargoes to ship can contact shipowners who have vessels to carry the cargoes, both parties operating through agents. Like several British financial institutions, the Baltic Exchange has its origin in the seventeenth-century coffee houses, where merchants would meet to drink coffee, read newspapers and transact business. It is known as the Baltic Exchange because in the seventeenth century most of its business was with countries bordering the Baltic Sea.

Business is carried out on the trading floor, where chartering agents, representing those who have cargoes, and brokers, representing those who have ships, make oral agreements. However, this method of doing business has been affected by modern communications and now many agreements are made by telephone or telex, and the agents and brokers spend more time in their offices than on the trading floor.

The traditional business of the Baltic Exchange has been the chartering of tramp ships for specific voyages, but this type of business has been in decline in recent years. The growth area has been in container traffic run by shipping lines, and in bulk carriers, which are often chartered directly from their owners. Therefore, the Baltic Exchange has diversified into other areas, both shipping and non-shipping. The 750 member firms, with their 2,500 individual members, are often shipowners themselves and are involved in all aspects of shipping, such as the sale and purchase of ships, and the running of shipping services for large industrial companies which import and export raw materials (eg iron ore, oil).

The Baltic Exchange also functions as a commodity market for grain, potatoes and meat, and is involved in air chartering. It is an important invisible export earner, contributing about £300 million a year to the UK's Balance of Payments.

**Exercise 7.17**
*Things to find out*

Find out about the following topics and report what you have learnt in writing or as a short talk.

a   different types of merchant ships
b   air transport

# UNIT EIGHT *Revision and consolidation*

In this second revision unit you will have further practice in writing order letters and replies to order letters. There is also more practice with telexes, packing instructions, making notes and oral summaries.

## Exercise 8.1 *Letter writing*

The New Art Manufacturing
Company Ltd
96-98 Wood Lane
Chiswick
London
W5A 3EU

Tel: 01 779 2323
Cables: NEWART
Telex: 375232
VAT Registration No 161 4269 64

A. Ferguson & Sons
Timber Merchants
The Longman Estate
Inverness
Scotland

Order Form:  99861

| Quantity | Description | Price |
|---|---|---|
| 5,000 | Pine Planks<br>First Grade Quality<br>3000mm x 400mm | £8,750 per 1,000 |
| 1,000 | Blockboards<br>A Grade<br>1000mm x 1000mm | £2,000 per 1,000 |

Date:     22 October 19--

Payment: Giro transfer

Signature:

*John, please write a letter to go with this order form (original attached)*
*GD.*

103

### Exercise 8.2
*Letter writing*

Read this note and write
an appropriate letter.

> 8pm
> Friday, 25 October 19—
>
> Alec,
>
> I've sent off part of the New Art order - all the blockboards and 3,000 pine planks. We can't send the other 2,000 until Monday when they arrive from the mill. Better explain that to them. I didn't have time to ask Betty to type the invoice.
>
> Tom

### Exercise 8.3
*Writing a telex*

Read this telex and memo and write an appropriate telex. Who will you send the telex to?

```
643792 MONTIMP M

185271 WINDSFAS G

89 03 21

ATTN JANET NOBLE

RE ORDER 7237 SILK DRESSES

PLS WRAP DRESSES INDIVIDUALLY IN PAPER AND PLYTHN PCK IN WDN BXS WITH
WTRPRF AND FRPRF LINING STNLS KP DRY DSTN VERA CRUZ NUMBER BXS ONE
TO TEN FIN

LAURA SANTAMARINA

185273 WINDSFAS G

643792 MONTIMP M
```

## Memo

To : **Kate Ross**

Date: **10th April**

Reference: **SDM 7237**

From : **Janet Noble**

Subject : **SILK DRESSES (MEXICAN ORDER)**

This order is late so I've arranged for despatch by air, not sea. The flight number is BA127 arriving in Mexico City at 10am on 14 April. The dresses will be wrapped in polythene and hung on racks. Please telex customer to inform. Could you accompany the dresses to Heathrow and check how they're loaded?

**Exercise 8.4**
*Making a list*
*Oral summary*

a  Find one sentence in this article which sums up Mr Ribbens's advice to salesmen.

b  List the gestures and positions, and the meanings Mr Ribbens says they have.

c  Give an oral summary of what you have read.

# Learn Body Language expert tells salesmen

WHEN salesmen lose an order, it could be the result of a failure in body language, rather than what the salesman has said.

'A smile, a gesture with the hand or a meaningful standing position is a neglected area of the salesmen's skills,' says Mr Geoffrey Ribbens, a senior lecturer at Slough College of Education's Management Centre.

'He can be more persuasive, establish better relations and be better understood if he uses correct and appropriate body positions and hand gestures,' he adds. But he emphasises that body language is a complex issue and should not be taken out of context. Rapid rubbing of the hands, for example, may merely mean that your hands are cold, and have no special significance.

He advises against displaying dominant body positions, such as standing too upright, or with your hands on your hips and your elbows sticking out. This would suggest too much confidence and dominance.

The salesman should smile when meeting customers and raise his eyebrows, then estimate the physical distance between himself and the customer. An acceptable distance in Western Europe is an arm's length, but an elbow length is suitable in the Mediterranean, and closer contact is acceptable in Eastern Europe.

A close watch should be kept on the body language of the customer. If a customer covers his mouth or touches his nose, this may indicate that he is thinking, not telling you the truth, thinks he has been insulted, or thinks you are lying.

Salesmen should also be careful about how they relax with the customer. Crossing your legs in a relaxed manner in front of an American could be regarded as rather effeminate. When people use their hands to express an idea and the palms are turned up, this indicates a sense of vagueness. Turned down they indicate firmness. An open palm indicates truth, honesty, and even, in some cases, submission. 'Therefore a salesman should reinforce his honesty by using the palms up sign,' says Mr Ribbens.

Chin-stroking indicates that a decision is being made. Fingertips touching to make a tent-shape 'indicates a confident attitude'.

When addressing an audience, persuasiveness can be increased by the open body position – arms and legs outward, a more upright position, and frequent head nods and hand gestures.

**Exercise 8.5**   Use the words listed below to complete the following memo.

---

# Memo ▮▮▮▮▮▮▮▮▮▮▮▮▮▮▮▮▮▮

**To :**   Brian Sharp                                **Date:**   21st May 19-

                                            **Reference:**

**From :**   Nigel Parkinson - for information only

**Subject :**   Order for Berber carpets - B3434/H

I have examined the _____(1) received from Eastern Carpets and am
convinced that they meet our _____(2).   The prices _____(3) are
also satisfactory and there is a good discount on _____(4) orders.
Mr Hassan, the London _____(5) of Eastern Carpets has assured me
that his company can meet our 1st November _____(6), and this has
been _____(7) in writing by his head office.

I have already given our packing _____(8) to Mr Hassan and he has
_____(9) me that  his company will use a freight _____(10) who
_____(11) in the _____(12) of goods to the United Kingdom.

According to our sales figures for the last _____(13) the demand for
this type of carpet is rising.   Therefore, we may be able to _____(14)
our next order.

---

| | |
|---|---|
| forwarder | specialises |
| samples | instructions |
| assured | bulk |
| confirmed | double |
| representative | requirements |
| despatch | quoted |
| quarter | deadline |

**Exercise 8.6**  **a**  Make a list of the difficulties of starting your own business
*Making a list*     as described in this article.
*Oral summary*  **b**  Give an oral summary of what you have read.

# Four profitable ways to go it alone

IF YOU want to go into business, you can start a company, buy one, buy into one or take out a franchise. Your choice will be governed by your money and your skills.

It is difficult to start a full-time business from scratch even if you have already used your skills in your spare time. You may not make as much money as you expected. It can take two or three years to establish a business and in your financial calculations you have to add the cost of your own living expenses until the business is established. Working from home would lower your expenses but could present all sorts of problems. It may disrupt home life, the house may be unsuitable, you may not be allowed to use your home for business purposes and you are never able to 'leave the office' and 'go home'.

If you choose to buy an existing small business, most are bought and sold through a business transfer agent, who would be able to offer you a number of choices and help you to borrow money to cover most of the purchase price.

You could buy into a business as a partner, but even if you have known the owners as friends, you will not have known them as business partners, and ought to regard them as strangers and get professional advice. You ought to under-stand your future position in the business and make sure that it is in writing. Oral agreements often arise between people who think that friendship will overcome any difficulties. In practice, friendship makes problems even worse.

Buying into a business by purchasing shares is a much more difficult area and should never be attempted without good professional advice. To be made a company director in return for your investment might sound marvellous, but if your share purchase was less than fifty per cent of the ordinary share capital of the company, your future as an employee or director would not be certain and could be ended.

Many customers of franchise businesses such as Kentucky Fried Chicken, Budget Cars and Holiday Inns, have no knowledge of their ownership. In each case a franchise is granted by the owner and is controlled by a contract which says precisely how the franchise should be run.

The arrangements are obviously good for the owner of the franchise as he can set up a network of businesses from which income is drawn using other people's capital. If you obtain a franchise you are working for the owner as well as yourself.

Nevertheless, the better franchises seem to offer a means of going into self-employment with a considerable chance of success. You would be running a business based on an established procedure and selling goods or offering services which are already well-known to the public. Running a well-organised franchise is like managing a branch of a large organisation except that there is a very strong personal involvement and the final profit or loss belongs to the person who has taken out the local franchise.

A franchise offering some kind of manual service to the public might require only an initial setting-up capital of £10–£15,000, but a fast food business would need very much more – probably £50–£100,000.

One important aspect of a good franchise is that you and your staff would receive complete training in running the business. This would be followed by continuous supervision to maintain standards and solve problems. At the same time the owners would be watching to see that you were honouring the contract and paying royalties.

Great care should be taken before investing a large sum in a franchise which has not existed, successfully, for a long time. You could be involved in establishing someone else's business with your capital.

# UNIT NINE

**Exercise 9.1**  Here is a letter of complaint from Robert Hart of Marlin Electronics. Read it carefully and answer the questions that follow.

Marlin Electronics
3 Atlantic Square
Toronto
Ontario
Canada
M4V 2Z2

Tel: 617 3344
Cables: MARLEX
Telex: 0525134 MARL

Mrs M Corbett
Sales Manager
Techno Products plc
30 Thorpe Way
Manchester
MN1 3RT
United Kingdom

Your ref:  MC/AF
Our ref: RH/32

30 June 19-

Dear Mrs Corbett

Our order No 3151 Video Scanners

I am writing with reference to the above order for security video
scanners, which we received today.

Seven of the cases contained the correct merchandise, which arrived
in good condition.  However, I have to inform you that case number 6
contained security alarms instead of security video scanners.  I can
only assume that your forwarding agent made a mistake, and the contents
of this case were intended for another customer.

I must ask you to arrange for the immediate despatch of replacements,
as we have firm orders from our own customers for the entire consignment.

I enclose a list of the contents of case number 6, which we will keep
in our warehouse until we receive instructions from you.

Yours sincerely

Robert Hart

Robert Hart
Chief Buyer

**Check your understanding**
a  Why is Mr Hart complaining?
b  Why is this an urgent matter?
c  What do you think will happen to the contents of case number 6?
d  Does Mr Hart sound angry?

## UNIT NINE

**Exercise 9.2**

Work in groups of two or three.
Mr Hart is complaining about the wrong goods being delivered.
What other reasons for complaint could there be?

*Focus on functions:*
*What should you say in a*
*letter of complaint?*

**A**  These functions are in the WRONG order. Match them with the sentences in Mr Hart's letter and list them in the CORRECT order.

**1**  State action taken by your company.
**2**  Refer to order.
**3**  Suggest possible causes of the problem.
**4**  State action(s) you require the other company to take.
**5**  State reason for complaint.

**B**  Match these sentences with your list of functions.

**a**  The goods have been placed in our warehouse.
**b**  There seems to have been . . .
**c**  We will keep the goods until . . .
**d**  I am writing about/concerning . . .
**e**  I regret to inform you that . . .
**f**  It appears that the boxes were . . .
**g**  I would like to inform you that . . .
**h**  We enclose a report on the damage from . . .
**i**  I must insist that you . . .
**j**  In accordance with our contract, I must ask you to . . .

**Exercise 9.3**
*Focus on punctuation:*
*The apostrophe – part two*

Notice where apostrophes are used, or not used, in these examples:

MISSING LETTERS

It's the first time we've placed an order with Smallwoods.
We'd better renew our insurance policy with Lloyd's.

SPELLING

There are two m's and two s's in 'commission'.

NUMBERS

There are two 8's after the decimal point.
The company was founded in the 1950s.
These envelopes are sold in 100s.

# UNIT NINE

### ABBREVIATIONS

There are several L/Cs to be checked.
Most of our managers are MBAs.

Now punctuate these sentences.

a   theyve put two 5s after the oblique
b   theyd prefer the screws packed in 100s rather than 1000s
c   there are two cs in accident
d   mps from all parties visited the factory
e   production of the ad/42s ceased in the early 1980s

**Exercise 9.4**
*Letter for dictation*

Sr P Hernandez, Manager, Merida Electronica, Avenida Principal, Miraflores, Caracas, Venezuela, has recorded the following letter for you to write. Write the address of his company as a letter heading, then listen to the cassette and write the letter.

**Exercise 9.5**
*Letter writing*

When David Jackson, Chief Buyer of Silver Office Supplies Ltd, returned from lunch, he found this telephone message on his desk.

---

*TELEPHONE MESSAGE*

MESSAGE FOR : *David Jackson*       TAKEN BY : *Molly*

NAME OF CALLER : *Barry Smith*       DATE : *26th April*

COMPANY NAME &
TELEPHONE NUMBER : *(Warehouse)*       TIME : *1.50 pm*

*SCROLL ups have arrived. 59 cases O.K. – no problems.
But one case contains the SCROLL 1000, not the 2000*

---

Prepare a letter of complaint to Shonan Computers, for David Jackson to sign. Use the list of functions on page 109 to help you.

**Exercise 9.6**
*Letter writing: formal and informal register*

A message from Paul West, Chief Salesman for Silver Office Supplies, and a good friend of David Jackson.

---

Dave,

You weren't in when I dropped by. I just wanted to have a word with you about these Protecta dust-covers from Perfect Plastics (what a misnamed company!) We just can't get rid of them. To put it bluntly our customers think they're rubbish (and so do I). They never take any more after they've had the first lot, and often send them back. There are hundreds still dumped at the back of our warehouse.

The trouble is they keep falling off the keyboards – they just won't stay put. That's because they're very poorly designed. On top of that when they hit the floor, even a carpeted floor, they shatter like glass. They're really no good at all, and they're giving us a bad name.

Can't you get the company to take them back? Can't we get our money back or swap them for plastic wallets – they're o.k., sell like hot cakes in fact. The Protecta dust-covers look nothing like the picture in the catalogue by the way.

Paul.

---

Here are some of the phrases David Jackson used in his letter to Perfect Plastics plc, 20 Burnham Way, Livingstone, Scotland AB1 2ED.

Match the phrases David Jackson uses with the informal expressions in Paul's note.

**a**   ... with reference to ...
**b**   ... have proved to be one of the less popular items in our range ...
**c**   ... our stocks are still high ...
**d**   ... Moreover, ...
**e**   ... our customers do not speak highly of them, and neither do our salesmen ...
**f**   ... I have to point out that ...
**g**   ... credit against our order for plastic wallets ...
**h**   ... with which we are entirely satisfied ...
**i**   ... are extremely fragile ...

**j** . . . to return the goods . . .

**k** . . . request a refund . . .

**l** . . . a small number of re-orders and many returned orders . . .

**m** . . . are not suitable for our customers' needs . . .

**n** . . . it seems that they do not fit very well owing to a design fault . . .

**o** . . . the illustration in your catalogue is rather misleading . . .

**p** . . . difficult to maintain our reputation as a supplier of top-quality goods . . .

**q** . . . which are in great demand . . .

Now write the complete letter to Perfect Plastics plc.

**Exercise 9.7**
*How to say it*

This is how these symbols are said:

| | | | |
|---|---|---|---|
| + | plus | × | multiplied by |
| − | minus | ∴ | therefore |
| > | more than | = | equals |
| < | less than | 3.25 | three point two five |
| ÷ | divided by | | |

Work with a partner.

Read Paula Armstrong's notes on her expenses.

Re-write and lay out this information in a form which she could submit to the accounts department of her company.

EXPENSES — Trip to Scotland                    3.11 – 6.11

Air Fare – (<train or car) £46

Hotel – ROYAL ABERDEEN, bill attached – £30 per night × 3 incl brkfst + dnr + £5 single room supplement × 3
total =
+ lunches £15 + £20 + £45

Car hire – £20 per day × 3
+ 100 miles @ 6·5p per mile
+ £7 petrol
+ VAT @ 15% on total (except petrol)

Helicopter Hire – £240 per day ÷ 6 (six passengers) ∴ my share =

– £200 cash allowance received.

# UNIT NINE

Read the passage about insurance. Copy the passage into your notebooks, completing it with the correct words. Some words are used more than once.

| | | | |
|---|---|---|---|
| cover | claim | broker | return |
| risk | proposal form | underwriter | compensation |
| policy | premium | claims form | commission |

**Insurance: What it is and how it works**

Export consignments can be stolen, damaged or even totally destroyed in transit, causing financial loss to the exporter. To protect themselves against such r_____s (1), exporters always insure their consignments. Without this insurance c_____ (2), a company could even be put out of business by the loss of a large consignment. With this insurance _____ (3), the insurance company will pay c _____ (4) for the loss and the exporting company will be able to stay in business.

To insure a cargo, exporting companies pay a small percentage of the value to the insurance company. These p_____s (5) will create a pool of money that can be used to pay the minority of companies who suffer loss and c_____ (6) compensation. In this way, the r_____ (7) is spread and people have a sense of security. The insurance company expects to receive more money in p_____s (8) than it pays out in c_____s (9). Insurance companies have large amounts of money, the p_____ (10) income, to invest, and the r_____ (11) on their investments increases the size of the pool of money from which they pay _____ (12) to policyholders who make claims.

When insurance is taken out, a p_____ f_____ (13) is completed, which gives details of what is insured, for how long and the nature of the risk. U_____s (14), who work for the insurance company, then assess the r_____ (15) and calculate the _____ (16) – the price of insurance. The client then receives the po_____ (17), which is the contract between the insured and the insurer, giving full details of c_____ (18) and c_____ (19).

Instead of going directly to an insurance company, it is possible to seek advice from an insurance b_____ (20) about the many different po_____s (21) available from insurance companies. The b_____ (22) is paid c_____ (23) by the insurance company whose p_____ (24) is chosen.

# UNIT NINE

**Exercise 9.9**    Abacus Laboratory Equipment Ltd has recently experienced several minor and some major disasters. What kind of insurance should Abacus have taken out to protect themselves against the risk of these things happening? Look at the things that happened to Abacus and study the table that shows the different types of insurance that are available.

Work with a partner.
Match the type of insurance to the incidents that occurred.

**a** WAREHOUSE INFERNO

Firemen fought a blaze at Abacus Ltd for over two hours yesterday. Over £5,000 of the stock was destroyed. It is believed that the fire started in the workers rest-room.

**b** MEMO _____

**From:** M Jones
**To:**    D Wilson, Chief Accountant
....unfortunately, J M Martin & Sons, who owe us £10,000, have gone out of business....virtually no chance of recovering the money......

**c** GENERAL WORKERS UNION

Dear Sir,
.....our members, Mr K Brown and Mr L Gordon, employed by you as warehousemen, were badly injured when a pile of boxes collapsed on top of them....intend to take legal action .....compensation for injuries......

**d** ABACUS

Dear Mr Morrison,

Order No. 12576/C
... regret to inform you that we are unable to deliver owing to a fire in our warehouse which ...

**e** THIEVES STRIKE AGAIN

There was another break-in at the premises of Abacus Ltd on Saturday, despite the recent installation of an alarm system. Apart from the loss of valuable electronic equipment, considerable damage was done.

**f** HARKER & HARKER, SOLICITORS

Dear Sirs,
.....our client, while visiting your offices, was injured in an accident involving a glass door....inadequate lighting..... intend to start legal proceedings.......

114

**g**

TELEPHONE MESSAGE
DATE: Tuesday, 5th May
TIME: 4pm
TAKEN BY: Sarah

Bob (one of our drivers) phoned from Dover. Lorry destroyed by fire – export load completely lost.

**h**

### WYNN OUT OF THE COUNTRY

Mr Geoffrey Wynn, formerly Chief Accountant of Abacus Ltd, is believed by police to be living abroad. Last March, Mr Wynn disappeared, and so did £250,000 of his company's money . . . . . . .

### TYPES OF INSURANCE

| | |
|---|---|
| FIRE | this covers the risk of fire, but can also include cover against explosion, flooding, earthquake and other risks to property. |
| CONSEQUENTIAL LOSS | this covers the loss of business caused by accidents, eg, if a company cannot produce goods to fulfil an order because machinery has been destroyed in a fire. |
| THEFT | this covers loss or damage due to the activities of thieves. |
| EMPLOYERS' LIABILITY | if an employee has an accident at work, he may claim compensation from the company for his injuries. This kind of insurance provides cover against this possibility. |
| PUBLIC LIABILITY | if a member of the public has an accident on the company's premises, he may claim compensation from the company. |
| FIDELITY BOND | this protects the company against acts of dishonesty by its own employees. |
| BAD DEBTS | this protects the company against the risk that its customers will not pay. |
| MOTOR VEHICLE | this must cover all risks associated with the use of vehicles. |
| GOODS/CASH IN TRANSIT | this covers goods and cash being transported from one place to another. |

## UNIT NINE

**Exercise 9.10**  SHOULD HAVE + PAST PARTICIPLE — failure to do essential things
MUST HAVE + PAST PARTICIPLE — making deductions

Abacus suffered financial loss from these incidents because it did not do things that were essential. It was essential to renew their fire insurance, but they didn't do that.

We can say: They should have renewed their fire insurance.
OR        They shouldn't have forgotten to renew their fire insurance.
OR        The fire insurance policy should have been renewed.

Work with a partner.
Look at the list of incidents on pages 114–115. Make a list of the things Abacus should and should not have done.

What do you think were some of the probable reasons for these incidents? Make deductions from the information given on pages 114–115.

We can say about the accident
in the warehouse:   Someone must have stacked the boxes too high.
OR        The workers must have been careless.
OR        They must have ignored the safety regulations.

 **Exercise 9.11**
*Listen to this*  Listen to Janet and Elizabeth talking about an accident that has occurred in the office. Copy the accident report form into your notebook and complete it.

**Accident Injury Report Form EA/ARF/6/88**

*This report form is only to be used for accidents in the office.*

**DETAILS OF ACCIDENT**

Date of accident: ...............................................................................

Time of accident ...............................................................................

Exact location: ...............................................................................

Were the following informed?    a)  rnanagement            YES/NO*
                                            b)  safety representative      YES/NO*

Number of casualties ...............................................................................

What happened? (*Please include details of any plant, equipmem,
                  furniture etc. involved, any contributory factors,
                  and what any injured person was doing.*)

...............................................................................

...............................................................................

...............................................................................

Name(s) and status of witness(es) of accident: ...............................................

...............................................................................

**DETAILS OF INJURED PERSON**

Name: ...............................................................................

Address: ...............................................................................

Age: ...............................................................................

Male ☐    Female ☐

Job title: ...............................................................................

Injury details (*nature and part of body*) ...............................................

...............................................................................

...............................................................................

Ambulance summoned/taken or sent to hospital/doctor
summoned/first aid only/advised to see doctor/no action taken*

Was injured person kept in hospital for over 24 hours?            YES/NO*

Normal hours of work of injured person:            FROM ...... TO ......

Actual hours worked:            FROM ...... TO ......

Length of absence: Nil/still absent/ ...... days*

*circle as appropriate

Office Manager's signature: ...............................

Date: ...........................

**Exercise 9.12**     In this letter Mr Thomas, of Abacus Laboratory Equipment Ltd, enquires about insurance cover for a special consignment.

Laboratory Equipment Ltd
12-16 Castle Lane Newbury
Berks RG1 2CS

Tel: 0635 55467 Cables: ABLAB Telex: 546432 ABLE G

Registration Number: 2113986 England
Registered Office: 12 Castle Lane, Newbury, Berks RG1 2CS

```
Mr  J  Barrett                                 Our ref: JT/MS
Amalgamated Insurance plc
Beacon House
Ashingdown Road
Athelney
Sussex
SU2 AT1                                        2 November 19-


Dear Mr Barrett

I am writing to enquire about insurance cover for a consignment of
medical instruments which we are sending by sea to Montevideo, Uruguay.

The consignment will be leaving Tilbury on 1 December and arriving in
Montevideo on 14 December.  This consignment is exceptionally valuable -
£20,000 - and is not covered by our existing policy with you.  We
therefore request a premium quotation for this voyage only.  The goods
have been sold CIF Montevideo, so we require cover from our warehouse to
Montevideo dockside.

We look forward to receiving a competitive quotation, and you may contact
me by telephone if there is any further information that you require.

Yours sincerely


James Thomas
Managing Director
```

***Check your understanding***     **a**  Why do you think this consignment is not covered by the existing policy?

**b**  What further details might Mr Barrett want to know?

**c**  Does the customer in Montevideo need to insure these goods himself?

**Exercise 9.13**
*Listen to this*

Copy these headings into your notebooks.

CARGO DESTINATION TERMS TRANSPORT DEPARTURE DATE VALUE

Listen to Mr Thomas talking to his Personal Assistant about export consignments and make notes under the headings. Using this information, write to Mr Barrett of Amalgamated Insurance to enquire about insurance for the consignments mentioned. Use the model letter to help you.

**Exercise 9.14**
*Letter writing*

The following letter, a request for a claims form, was accidentally torn up. Look through all the pieces and then re-arrange them in the correct order.

Read the complete letter that you have written and list the three things that Mr Thomas does in this letter.

```
Dear Sirs          However          of this unfortunate incident

We write to inform you        Managing Director

General & Commercial Insurance plc        We would be grateful if
Tower House
Stamford Bridge Road
York
YO2 8TB                              policy No 234/R

and extinguished the fire                    Fortunately

has damaged £2,000 of stock        James Thomas

Yours faithfully

that a fire broke out in our storeroom            on 19 January

21 January 19-                        before it got out of control
```

ABACUS
Laboratory Equipment Ltd
12-16 Castle Lane Newbury
Berks RG1 2CS

Tel: 0635 55467 Cables: ABLAB Telex: 546432 ABLE G

Registration Number: 2113986 England
Registered Office: 12 Castle Lane, Newbury, Berks RG1 2CS

```
you would send us a claim form

    the combined effect of fire and water

on which we will give you full details

our sprinkler system came into operation
```

**Exercise 9.15**
*Listen to this*
Mary Stephens is working late in her office at Abacus Laboratories. She is just about to leave when the phone rings. Listen to the conversation and then:

**a** Write a short memo to Mr Thomas explaining what has happened.

**b** Write a letter, for Mr Thomas to sign, to Amalgamated Insurance, giving brief details of the incident and requesting a claims form.

## Lloyd's of London

Lloyd's of London is a famous and unique institution in the world of insurance. It is well-known for shipping insurance, but since the end of the nineteenth century it has accepted other business and today more than two-thirds of its £8,000 million a year premium income comes from non-marine business. It is important to realise that Lloyd's is not a company, but a market place where individuals transact business. It is an international market-place – over three-quarters of its premiums come from overseas.

Lloyd's began in the seventeenth century in a coffee-house owned by a Mr Edward Lloyd. At that time coffee-houses were popular meeting-places for businessmen, and Mr Lloyd's coffee-house soon became a place where marine insurance could be readily obtained from wealthy merchants who would underwrite risks to the the full extent of their personal wealth. They would write their names on a slip of paper under the description of the risk, and this is why they were called 'underwriters'. By the end of the eighteenth century Lloyd's had its own premises and in 1986 it moved into a new purpose-built building in the City of London.

Wealthy people who become members of Lloyd's expose their wealth to huge risks because there are no limits to the liability of members if losses occur. Members can lose all their money. However, normally premium income is in excess of the money paid out to meet claims and the profits are shared by the members. There are about 24,000 underwriting members of Lloyd's, and they are grouped into about 400 syndicates of various sizes. Most of these members, or underwriters, do not actually work at Lloyd's. Each syndicate has an underwriting agent, who does work there and accepts risks on behalf of the other members of his syndicate, or 'names' as they are called. To become a 'name', it is necessary to show that you have at least £100,000 of readily available assets, half of which must be deposited with Lloyd's. A member with £100,000 would be allowed to accept premiums of up to £200,000. This means that for each syndicate there is a maximum amount of premiums that it can accept. For this reason, the insurance risk of, say, a very expensive oil tanker, is shared by several syndicates, each one taking a percentage of the risk. In the late seventies and early eighties a few underwriting agents stole large amounts of money from members of their syndicates. They were expelled from Lloyd's and changes were made in the regulations and working practices.

Shipowners and others who are seeking insurance cannot approach underwriters directly, but must go through another kind of Lloyd's member – a Lloyd's broker – who, for a commission,

will arrange insurance with the underwriters. The broker has a slip of paper, describing the risk, which the underwriter signs, indicating the percentage of risk he or she is prepared to accept. A broker may have to approach many underwriters before the risk is completely covered, and some underwriters may refuse the risk entirely, but a broker, with his or her expert knowledge of the market will know the most suitable ones to approach. A Lloyd's broker may also place business with insurance companies, which are not part of Lloyd's.

In order to assess risk, it is necessary to have accurate information, and Lloyd's publishes a daily newspaper, 'Lloyd's List', which gives news about shipping and other forms of transport, and also several reference books. In addition, there are, all over the world, more than five hundred Lloyd's agents, who provide information about shipping movements and report on damaged vessels.

At Lloyd's there is a bell, salvaged from HMS Lutine in the nineteenth century. In the days before modern communications this was rung twice for good news and once for bad, but today it is mainly used on ceremonial occasions.

**Exercise 9.16**
*Things to find out*
Find out about one of the following topics and report what you have learnt in writing or as a short talk.

    **a**  insurance companies
    **b**  financial scandals
    **c**  bribery and corruption
    **d**  life insurance

# *UNIT TEN*

**Exercise 10.1**   Replies to letters of complaint are known as LETTERS OF ADJUSTMENT. Read Mrs Corbett's letter, about wrongly delivered goods, and answer the questions that follow.

# TECHNO PRODUCTS

Techno Products plc
30 Thorpe Way  Manchester MN1 3RT

Tel: 061 660 891 Cables: TECHPRO
Telex: 189227 TECH G Fax (group 3): 061 54541

A Company Registered in England: No 9916670
Registered Office: 2 Seacoal Lane, Manchester MN5 6CB

```
Mr Robert Hart
Chief Buyer
Marlin Electronics                 Your ref:  RH/32
3 Atlantic Square                  Our ref:  MC/EW
Toronto
Ontario
Canada
M4V 2Z2                            5 July 19-

Dear Mr Hart

Your order No 3151 for video scanners

We thank you for your letter of 30 June, in which you informed us that
case number 6 of the above consignment contained the wrong goods.

We have looked into this matter and discovered that there appears to
have been some confusion in the numbering of two different orders which
were collected by our forwarding agent for despatch to Canada.  We have
reviewed our coding system and can assure you that similar mistakes will
not happen again.

We have already despatched replacements for the contents of case number 6
and instructed our representative in Canada to collect the wrongly-
delivered goods as soon as possible.

Finally, we would like to apologise for the inconvenience you were
caused and to thank you for your patience in this matter.

We look forward to hearing of the safe arrival of the replacements and to
doing further business with you.

Yours sincerely

Margaret Corbett

Margaret Corbett (Mrs)
Sales Manager
```

# UNIT TEN

**Check your understanding**

a  Why have Techno written this letter?

b  What has Mrs Corbett found out about the packing of the goods?

c  What improvements has she made in despatch procedures?

d  Who will collect the contents of case number 6?

e  Read the letter again. Close your book and give an oral summary of the letter. Your partner will remind you of anything you miss out.

**Exercise 10.2**
*Focus on functions:*
*What should you say when*
*you reply to a complaint?*

A  These functions are in the WRONG order. Match them with the sentences in Mrs Corbett's letter and list them in the CORRECT order.

1  State action taken to prevent the problem happening again.

2  Acknowledge the letter of complaint.

3  Reassure the customer.

4  End optimistically.

5  State action taken to solve the immediate problem.

6  Explain the cause of the problem.

7  Apologise.

B  Match these sentences with your list of functions.

a  Your detailed description of the damage was very helpful to us.

b  I have authorised the despatch of replacements by air freight.

c  Please accept our apologies for the inconvenience.

d  We have arranged for the collection of the wrongly-delivered goods by . . .

e  We have investigated the matter and discovered that the mistake was due to . . .

f  You may be sure that such a mistake will not be made again.

g  Our new packing materials will prevent this kind of damage in future.

h  The new quality control procedures we have introduced will ensure that this problem does not happen again.

**Exercise 10.3**
*Focus on punctuation:*
*Putting extra information in*
*sentences*

commas , . . . . . . . . . ,
brackets ( . . . . . . . . )
dashes  – . . . . . . . . . –

can all be used for this purpose.

a  Mr James Turner, Production Manager of Techno Ltd, will be visiting our research and development unit on Thursday, 8th June.

b  This year's production figures (see attached graph for details) show a marked improvement on last year's. Brackets are used when the extra information is not part of the grammatical structure of the sentence.

c  Increases in the cost of raw materials – up by 50% so far this year – will inevitably lead to price increases for our customers.
Dashes are used to emphasise extra information which is surprising and important.

This memo has no punctuation at all. Re-write it, correctly laid-out and punctuated.

```
memo to mike miller from margaret corbett date 3rd april re kingston
electronics order no 4422 we have still not received payment from this
company i phoned mr cooper the managing director but he was unavailable
again we have written several times see attached correspondence without
getting a reply could you arrange a meeting with mr care our solicitor
as it is now time to take further steps firm action must be taken as our
unpaid invoices now totalling £90000 are causing us considerable
financial difficulties
```

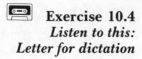

**Exercise 10.4**
*Listen to this:*
*Letter for dictation*

Mr A Suzuki, Sales Manager of Shonan Computers, has left a message on cassette for you to write. Put his company's name and address as a letter heading and then listen to the cassette and prepare the letter for his signature.

# UNIT TEN

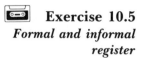

**Exercise 10.5**
*Formal and informal register*

Mrs Margaret Corbett, Sales Manager of Techno, left a message on cassette for her secretary. After listening to the message, her secretary wrote the letter on page 122.

Listen to the message.
Match the words used by Mrs Corbett with the words used in the letter.

For example:

Mrs Corbett says, 'I'm telling Mike Smith to pick up the goods they don't want.'

Her secretary writes, 'We have instructed our representative in Canada to collect the wrongly-delivered goods.'

Now match these sentences in the same way.

MRS CORBETT'S MESSAGE:

**a** We've just got this letter

**b** It's about the video scanners

**c** I've checked it out

**d** One of the boxes had the wrong stuff in it

**e** There's been a terrible muddle. They made a mess of the numbering.

**f** The replacements have already gone off

**g** I've changed the system so it can't happen again

**h** Say we are sorry for messing them about

THE LETTER:

**1** Case number 6 contained the wrong goods.

**2** We have already despatched replacements.

**3** We thank you for your letter of 30th June.

**4** We would like to apologise for the inconvenience you were caused.

**5** We have reviewed our coding system and can assure you that similar mistakes will not happen again.

**6** We have looked into this and discovered . . .

**7** Your order No. 3151 for video scanners

**8** There appears to have been some confusion in the numbering.

## UNIT TEN

**Exercise 10.6**
*Letter writing*

Ms Georgina Dickenson, Manager of the New Art Manufacturing Company Ltd, has asked you to draft a reply to this letter she has received from Kurt Schiller Gmb H, her customer in West Germany. She has made some notes on the letter to guide you. Your reply need not include all her comments.

---

... and eighteen of the sofa-beds arrived in good condition. However, we have to inform you that two arrived damaged and are in an unsaleable condition - the frames are broken, the covers torn and the stuffing is hanging out. — *quite a mess!*
*say we are sorry*

One of these crates arrived intact with no visible signs of damage to the

*comment generally on handling problems*

crate itself, which leads us to believe that damage occurred prior to the *unlikely - no idea how - I'm checking out procedures anyway* despatch of the goods. The other crate, however, was badly cracked and splintered, and there were signs that rats had got inside. *obviously damaged in transit*

*— send straightaway*

We must therefore insist on immediate replacements for the two damaged sofa-beds, and await your instructions as to how you wish to dispose of ... *Keep for inspection - t.b.a.*

---

**FAX – What it is and how it works**

- FAX is the abbreviation for facsimile machine. It is a machine that transmits an image of a document via the international telephone network. If you place a letter in a FAX machine in London, it can be transmitted to Tokyo, where another FAX machine will print out an exact copy of your letter.

- Facsmile machines were invented as long ago as 1901, but until recently were used mainly for transmitting newspaper photographs and weather maps. The earily FAX machines were large, noisy, expensive and very slow. In recent years, however, FAX machines have become more and more popular. This is because the use of digital technology, the same type of technology that is used in computers and word processors, has enabled the machines to be much smaller, quieter, cheaper and faster. Modern machines can transmit an A4 document in as little as twelve seconds. Moreover, there is an agreed international standard for FAX machines, which means that machines made by different manufacturers are compatible. One of the major advantages of FAX machines is that they can transmit not just printed words but pictures, diagrams, handwriting and signatures. They can be used to transmit the documents used in foreign trade.

● FAX machines have a light-sensitive scanner which distinguishes between light and dark, eg black print on white paper. This information is converted into digital pulses which are sent down the telephone line. The receiving FAX machine interprets this information and re-creates the image, which is then printed out on paper.

**Exercise 10.7**
*Points for discussion*

a In which kinds of business are FAX machines particularly useful?

b Are FAX machines useful for private individuals? Is it worth having one at home?

c If FAX becomes even more popular, what effect might this have on postal services? telex?

**Exercise 10.8**
*Focus on vocabulary*

rise rose risen
raise raised raised
arise arose arisen
rise (noun)

Notice how these words are used in the following sentences:

*Techno have raised their prices by 10%.*
*The price we pay for our raw materials has risen by 30% this year.*
*Mrs Corbett has been given a 20% rise in salary.*
*A problem has arisen in the development of the new satellite dish.*

Complete these sentences with the correct form of the right word.

a Several difficulties have _____ in our negotiations over the new contract.

127

**b** Last year our productivity was 100 units per month per worker, but this year it has _____ to 120 units per month per worker.

**c** We will have to _____ the prices of at least two of the models in our range.

**d** Our turnover is expected to _____ from £20,000 per month to £25,000 per month.

**e** Last month the interest rate that we pay on our bank loan _____ from 12% to 15%.

**f** It was expected that the _____ in profits would be greater than 8%.

**Exercise 10.9**
*Listen to this:*
*Reporting what you have*
*heard at meetings*

You have recently attended a meeting at which the Chairman of your company gave some important information in the form of a short speech.

You must note pieces of information from the Chairman's speech.

**a** Use your notes to complete the information in the table of statistics, and the graph. Draw a bar chart for THIS year.

**b** Make a short oral report to your colleagues, in which you tell them the main points that the Chairman made and explain the information in the table, graph and chart.

Draw a bar chart for this year according to the information given by the Chairman.

| | Last Year | | This Year | |
|---|---|---|---|---|
| Turnover (total sales) | Total £200,995,336 | | Total **4** | |
| | Domestic 110,443,003 | Export 90,552,333 | Domestic **5** | Export **6** |
| Profit | Gross | Net | Gross | Net |
| | **2** | 12,532,800 | **1** | 10,806,127 |
| Interest on Loans | 1,360,000 | | **3** | |
| Employees | 1800 | | **8** | |
| Output: Satellite Dishes | 190 | | **7** | |
| Video Scanners | 5000 | | 5500 | |

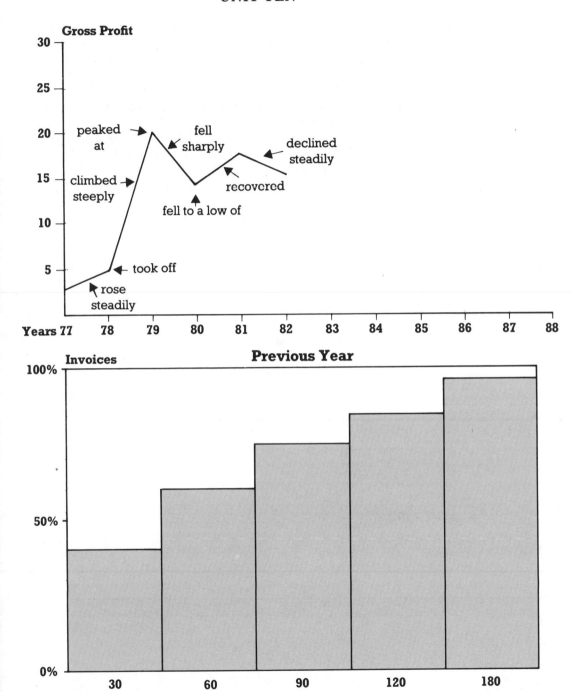

**Gross Profit**

peaked at

climbed steeply

rose steadily

took off

fell sharply

fell to a low of

recovered

declined steadily

**Years** 77 78 79 80 81 82 83 84 85 86 87 88

**Previous Year**

**Invoices**

100%

50%

0%

30 60 90 120 180

**Paid within – days**

**Exercise 10.10**
*Letters about*
*non-payment*

You will remember that Techno supplied satellite dishes to Kingston Electronics, Australia (see page 93). Read these questions and find the answers in the three letters that follow.

**a** What are the letters about?

**b** In what ways are they the same? In what ways are they different?

**c** These letters were written on the following dates: 28th October, 14th December, 7th February. Which date goes with which letter?

**d** Which words express the most polite request for payment?

**e** Which words set a deadline for payment?

LETTER A

Dear Mr Cooper

Your order (No 412) for satellite dishes

We are writing to remind you that we have not yet received payment for this order.

As you must realise, it is not possible for us to continue to supply goods on such favourable terms unless our customers clear their accounts promptly.

We have not had any explanation from you concerning your reasons for this delay, or any indication of when you intend to settle the account, despite our reminder.

We therefore have to ask you to notify us immediately of the arrangements you are making for payment.

Yours sincerely

*Margaret Corbett*

Margaret Corbett   (Mrs)
Sales Manager

# *UNIT TEN*

Dear Mr Cooper

Your order (No 412) for satellite dishes

We refer to the invoice for the above order which we sent to you by air mail on 14 June.

According to the terms of the invoice, settlement of this account was to be made within ninety days.  However, we do not appear to have received payment from you.  In case you did not receive the original invoice, we enclose a copy with this letter.

As payment is now overdue, we would be grateful if you would arrange for early settlement.

Yours sincerely

*Margaret Corbett*

Margaret Corbett (Mrs)
Sales Manager

Dear Mr Cooper

Your order (No 412) for satellite dishes

You have still not given us any explanation for your failure to clear this account.

We have been very patient and have made every effort to maintain a good business relationship with you.  However, if we do not receive payment by the end of this month, we shall have no alternative but to place the matter in the hands of our solicitors, who will take the necessary steps to secure payment.

Yours sincerely

*Margaret Corbett*

Margaret Corbett (Mrs)
Sales Manager

## UNIT TEN

**Exercise 10.11**
*Letter writing*

Study the invoice and the memo and write an appropriate letter.

---

# Memo ████████████████████████████

To : *Mike Miller*                                    Date: *15 November 19—*

                                                          Reference:

From : *Margaret Corbett*

Subject : *Unpaid invoice - Wellington Farmers Co-operative*

*I'm very concerned about this unpaid invoice (see attached documents). We telexed them on 30th September, but there there has been no response. Although we've been trading with them for the last five years and they've always settled their accounts promptly, this order is by far the biggest they've ever placed. Could you chase it up immediately?*

---

**INVOICE**

| | |
|---|---|
| **Seller**<br>Techno Products plc<br>30 Thorpe Way<br>Manchester<br>United Kingdom | **Notify**<br>Wellington Farmers Cooperative<br>50/52 Happy Valley Road<br>Wellington<br>New Zealand |
| **Consignee**<br>To Order | **Buyer (if not consignee)**<br>Wellington Farmers Cooperative<br>50/52 Happy Valley Road<br>Wellington<br>New Zealand |

Invoice No.  85541      Date.12th August 19—
Sellers Reference      85541
Buyers Reference      Contract 6715
Country of Origin      United Kingdom
Country of Destination  New Zealand
Vessel/Aircraft      S.S. Amethyst
Port of Loading      Tilbury
Port of Discharge  Wellington
Terms of Delivery & Payment
        CIF Wellington
        Open Account- within 30 days

| Marks & Numbers, Number and kind of packages, Description of Goods | Quantity | Amount |
|---|---|---|
| 5 cases of electric shears in accordance with contract number 6715 dated 29th July 19—<br><br>Stencils 1-5 WFC WELLINGTON | | |

We certify the electric shears are in accordance with contract No: 6715 dated 29th July 19— between Techno Products Ltd and Wellington Farmers Cooperative.

It is hereby certified that this invoice shows the actual price of the goods, that no other invoice has or will be issued, and that all particulars are true and correct.

Name of Signatory  M. Corbett
Place and Date    Manchester, 12 August 19—
Signature
    *Margaret Corbett*

| | |
|---|---|
| Total | £25,000 |
| Gross Weight | 500 kg |
| Cube M3 | 5 |

**Exercise 10.12**
*Describing cause and effect –*
*Consequently, Due to, As,*
*Because*

Read this passage, which is about technology and work, and note down all the causes and effects, in the way shown by the examples. You should be able to find six more. Pay special attention to the words which link cause and effect.

development of steam powered machinery (cause)»» rapid growth of factories (effect)

homeworkers unable to compete (cause)»» forced out of business and became employees (effect)

Technology has a great influence on where, as well as how, people live and work. For example, the development of steam-powered machinery in the eighteenth century resulted in the rapid growth of factories. Because homeworkers were unable to compete with the production capacities of the new factories, they were forced out of business and became employees in the factories. As a consequence of the introduction of steam-powered machinery, therefore, there was a clear separation of the workplace from the home.

One effect of the development of fast, affordable transport has been to free people from the necessity of living within walking distance of work. As a result of the expansion of the railways in the nineteenth century, for instance, many white collar workers were able to move to the clearer air of the suburbs and commute to their jobs in the city centres. The habit of travelling quite long distances to work has grown in the twentieth century due to the availability of mass-produced reasonably-priced cars.

Recent developments in computerised communications systems, however, have led to speculation that homeworkers may once again become an important part of the workforce. By using a word processor linked to a personal computer and connected by telephone to the company's computer, it is possible to exchange the information required to do a wide variety of 'office' jobs at home. Consequently, for those with the necessary skills, the office can now be at their fingertips, instead of at the end of a road or rail journey. In other words, 'brainworkers' can now 'telecommute' from home rather than physically commute to the office.

**Exercise 10.13**

This paragraph speculates about the possible consequences of 'telecommuting' from the point of view of the company. Put one word in each space to connect the causes and effects.

One _____·(1) of 'telecommuting' would be that fewer employees would require office space. _____ (2) companies would not need such large offices as they do now they would be able to save money on overheads such as rent, insurance, lighting and heating. Moreover, _____ (3) 'telecommuters' do not spend time in an office, companies do not have to pay them just for being there, but only for the work they do. _____ (4), some companies are encouraging 'telecommuters' to become self-employed. Companies which have already experimented with this way of working have reported an increase in productivity of up to fifty per cent _____ (5) to the use of self-employed 'telecommuters'. This can also _____ (6) to further savings _____ (7) the self-employed are not entitled to benefits such as paid holidays.

**Exercise 10.14**
*Writing from notes*

What are the positive and negative consequences of telecommuting from the worker's point of view?
Make a list of points and organise them into the best order. Write a paragraph using linking words to connect the causes and effects.

Here are some ideas to help you.

| CAUSE | EFFECT |
|---|---|
| satellites provide a worldwide communications network | possible to telecommute from the Scottish Highlands or the Hawaiian Islands |
| telecommuters work from home | avoid stress of rush-hour travel – save time and money<br>isolated, lonely, more difficult to organise unions<br>need to provide workspace, light |
| telecommuters self-employed | free from nine to five routine<br>more time for family<br>need for self discipline |

**Exercise 10.15**
*Discussion*

What effect do you think telecommuting might have on:

a  cities
b  trade unions
c  the design of houses
d  family life

## Commodity markets

Commodity markets are markets where manufacturers can buy raw material such as wool, coffee, sugar, rubber, tea, copper and the other products of farms, plantations and mines around the world. The City of London is a very important world centre for commodity trading of all kinds and because of London's geographical position the London markets are open when the markets in both the United States and the Far East are open.

Different methods of trading are used according to the commodity, but the most common is the open outcry method in which brokers, representing buyers or sellers, stand in a ring and shout out the prices at which they are prepared to buy or sell. This is the method used at the London Metal Exchange, which deals in zinc, tin, nickel, aluminium, silver, lead and copper. However, as with other markets, the introduction of new technology is causing the traditional face-to-face trading methods to be abandoned and new screen-based techniques to be developed.

Commodities are bought and sold at a 'spot' price – for immediate delivery, or at a 'forward' or 'future' price for delivery at a certain time in the future, in three months' time for example. As well as manufacturers who require a commodity to make a product, eg a company that needs to buy sugar and cocoa to make chocolate, there are also speculators who do not intend to take delivery of the commodity – their aim is to make a profit out of fluctuations in price.

Money can also be regarded as a commodity and it is traded in the foreign exchange market. This is a telephone market, taking place in the dealing rooms of major banks, where currencies are bought and sold all over the world. Foreign currencies and other financial contracts can also be traded on the floor of the London International Financial Futures Exchange.

**Exercise 10.16**
*Things to find out*  Find out about one of these topics and report what you have learnt in writing or as a short talk.

    **a**  Foreign Exchange
    **b**  A commodity market in your own country
    **c**  An important raw material, eg, oil, gold, copper, iron.

# UNIT ELEVEN

**Exercise 11.1**
*Letter writing:*
*Layout and*
*punctuation*

Techno Products plc have received another order from
Kingston Electronics. In view of the previous correspondence
between these companies (see pages 130–131), how do you
think Techno will respond?

Test your knowledge of punctuation and layout by presenting
this letter as it was received by Mr Cooper.

```
techno products plc 30 thorpe way manchester mn13rt tel 061660891 cables
techpro telex189227 tech g fax group three 061 54541 mr thomas cooper managing
director kingston electronics 32 medina way canberra new south wales
australia your ref tc33 our ref jcms32 29th june 19- dear mr cooper your
order no 620 for satellite dish antennae we thank you for the above order
and confirm that we have now received payment for the satellite dishes
which we delivered to you last june unfortunately we are unable to supply
you with satellite dish antennae by the date which you requested in your
order we are already working at full capacity to satisfy the heavy demand
for this product and it is unlikely that we will be able to meet your order
for at least six months however if you are willing to pay in advance we would
be prepared to give your order priority and deliver by the date you request we
await your further instructions in this matter yours sincerely margaret
corbett mrs sales manager
```

**Exercise 11.2**
*Check your understanding*

**a** Why do you think that Mrs Corbett mentions the order
for satellite dishes?

**b** Does she reject the order for satellite dish antennae?

*Focus on functions:*
*What should you say when*
*you refuse an order?*

**A** These functions are in the WRONG order. List them in the
CORRECT order.

1 Suggest an alternative
2 Thank the customer for the order.
3 Say why you cannot meet the order.
4 Say that you cannot meet the order.

**B** Match these sentences with your list of functions.

**a** We can assure you that model No 2311 will be suitable for
your needs.

**b** We very much regret that we cannot . . .

**c**   Unfortunately, we can supply only part of your order.

**d**   Thank you for your order, No 88976A, which we received today.

**e**   Model No H4/011 is temporarily out of stock.

**f**   If you are willing to wait for a short period, we can supply you in four weeks' time.

**g**   Owing to heavy demand for these goods from our existing customers, we are unable to accept new orders at present.

**h**   This model has been discontinued and replaced by . . .

**i**   We are sorry to tell you that we are unable to supply the goods you have requested.

**j**   These items are only available in packs of one hundred.

**k**   Perhaps you would consider increasing your order to . . .

**l**   We are unable to offer as large a discount as you have requested.

**m**   We expect to have this item in stock in July.

**n**   The minimum order for this item is fifty.

**Exercise 11.3**
*Letter for dictation*

Mrs Margaret Corbett, Sales Manager of Techno Products, has recorded a letter for you to write. Write the name of her company as a letter heading, then listen to the cassette and write the letter.

**Exercise 11.4**
*Letter writing*

Mrs Corbett has asked you to write a reply to the letter on page 138, on which she has written some comments.

Match the notes written on the letter with the formal expressions that you will need to use in your letter.

**a**   . . . could you inform us if you have any connection with the Magic Lamp Company which previously traded from your address . . .

**b**   . . . we have to inform you that we only give discounts of more than 20% to customers with whom we have established a good, long-term trading relationship . . .

**c**   . . . it appears that you have consulted an old catalogue because the numbers and prices quoted by you are out of date . . .

**d**   . . . we therefore enclose our current catalogue and new price list . . .

**e**   . . . fourteen days is the minimum delivery time we require for this size of order . . .

Aladdin's Lighting Emporium
59-63 Bishops Row
Knightsbridge
London
SW1 3AP   Tel: 01 730 2955

Techno Products plc
30 Thorpe Way
Manchester
MN1 3RT

*Sounds familiar?
Same address as Magic Lamp
Company – remember the trouble they
caused two years ago. Getting money
out of them was like getting blood
out of a stone!
—See file ML/266*

Dear Sirs

We are a (well-established) retail lighting company in one of the most

prestigious shopping areas in London.  We have recently seen your

catalogue and we believe that several of your products would be very

popular with our customers.  We are therefore placing an initial order

for 2,000 Spotlights (catalogue no. SP15).  Our official order form

for these goods is enclosed.   *old catalogue - send new one
wrong price on order form.*

*not as big as they think*

*only for our
best customers*
Because of (the size of our order) we would expect a bulk order discount

of 10% in addition to the normal trade discount of 20% mentioned in

your catalogue.  Our suppliers normally allow us to settle our accounts   *who?*

*not on!*
on a quarterly basis, and we would expect similar credit arrangements

with you.   *they must be joking!*

*out of the question – 14 min.*
Delivery within ten days is essential, as we are experiencing a very

heavy demand for this type of product at present.

*No!*
We trust that these terms are acceptable to you as we expect to be

placing further large orders with you in future.

*Lets see how this goes first*

Yours faithfully

Andrew Daley
Manager

**f** . . . as to paying on a quarterly basis, this is a matter which would require further discussion . . .

**g** . . . should you wish to place a revised order when you have read our latest catalogue, please do not hesitate to contact us . . .

Now prepare a correctly laid-out and punctuated reply. The sentences above do not make up a complete letter. You will need to use some linking words and phrases.

**Exercise 11.5**
*Oral practice*
*Note taking*
*Letter writing*

Work with a partner.
You have received an order from Vortexlab Ltd. Look at their order form. Student A must check with the warehouseman (Student B) that these items are in stock. Student B should look at the stock list on page 140 and give Student A the required information. Student A should make notes on the information given.
Do you have in stock all the items that Vortexlab require?

What kind of letter should you write to Vortexlab?

Plan your letter and write it for Mr Thomas' signature.

---

ORDER FORM

```
Abacus Laboratory Equipment Ltd
12/16 Castle Lane
Newbury
Berks  RG1 2CS
England
```

# VORTEXLAB Ltd

Peak House
Peterport
Jersey

NO.  88976A                    DATE: 1st April 19--

| QUANTITY | DESCRIPTION OF ITEM | CATALOGUE NUMBER | PRICE |
|----------|--------------------|------------------|---------------------|
| 5 | Advanced Balance | 22M/09 | 287.90 ea |
| 20 | Advanced Microscope | M1/10 | 410.10 ea |
| 50 | Flask Brushes | CH7040 | 1.88 ea |
| 75 | 6mm Spring Clips | CH5776 | 1.75 (per pack) |
| 1 | Crucible Furnace | H4/011 | 35.60 ea |

SIGNED: *J Cook*

for Vortexlab

```
STOCK SHEET NO. 58  MARCH 31st

ITEM              CATALOGUE NO.     PRICE     NO. IN STOCK  COMMENTS

Advanced          22M/09            287.90    5             Re-ordered
Balance

Junior Balance    22M/06             99.32    67

Triple Beam       22M/03             96.90    89
Balance

Electronic        22M/010            54.00    30
Balance

Digital           13E/005            87.50    10
Plotter

Galvanometer      13E/006            34.85    50

Advanced          M1/10             410.00     0            50 on order
Microscope                                                  due May

Crucible          H4/011             35.60     0            Discontinued
Furnace                                                     New model
                                                            available
                                                            May

Flat bottom       CH7001              0.61    500
flask 100cm3

Flask, conical    CH7006              0.41    500
wide mouth

Flask, conical    CH7007              0.35    500
narrow mouth

Flask brushes     CH7040              1.88    500           minimum
                                                            order 100

6mm Spring        CH5776              1.75    980           available in
Clips                                (pack)                 packs of ten
                                                            only
```

**Exercise 11.6**
*Focus on vocabulary: Hire,*
*Rent, Let, Lease, Charter*

Notice how these words are used in the advertisements.
Can you work out the differences in meaning by studying the
details of the advertisements?

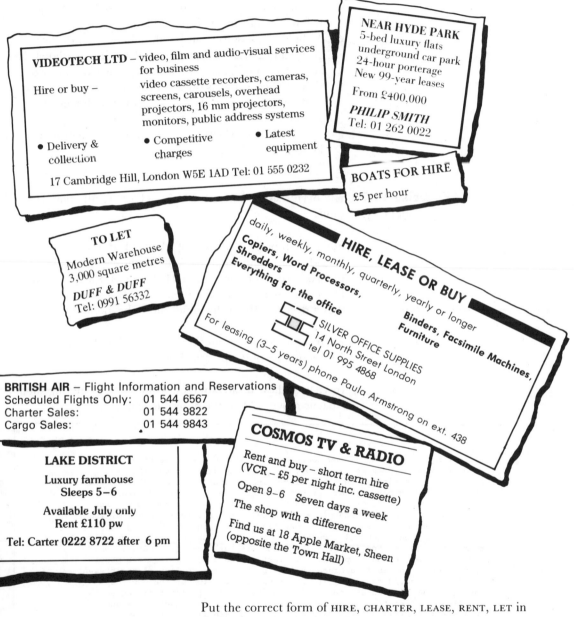

**VIDEOTECH LTD** – video, film and audio-visual services for business

Hire or buy – video cassette recorders, cameras, screens, carousels, overhead projectors, 16 mm projectors, monitors, public address systems

- Delivery & collection
- Competitive charges
- Latest equipment

17 Cambridge Hill, London W5E 1AD Tel: 01 555 0232

**NEAR HYDE PARK**
5-bed luxury flats
underground car park
24-hour porterage
New 99-year leases

From £400,000

*PHILIP SMITH*
Tel: 01 262 0022

**BOATS FOR HIRE**
£5 per hour

**TO LET**
Modern Warehouse
3,000 square metres

*DUFF & DUFF*
Tel: 0991 56332

**HIRE, LEASE OR BUY**
daily, weekly, monthly, quarterly, yearly or longer

Copiers, Word Processors, Shredders
Everything for the office

Binders, Facsimile Machines, Furniture

SILVER OFFICE SUPPLIES
14 North Street London
tel 01 995 4868

For leasing (3–5 years) phone Paula Armstrong on ext. 438

**BRITISH AIR** – Flight Information and Reservations
Scheduled Flights Only:    01 544 6567
Charter Sales:              01 544 9822
Cargo Sales:               .01 544 9843

**LAKE DISTRICT**

Luxury farmhouse
Sleeps 5–6

Available July only
Rent £110 pw

Tel: Carter 0222 8722 after 6 pm

**COSMOS TV & RADIO**

Rent and buy – short term hire
(VCR – £5 per night inc. cassette)

Open 9–6   Seven days a week

The shop with a difference

Find us at 18 Apple Market, Sheen
(opposite the Town Hall)

Put the correct form of HIRE, CHARTER, LEASE, RENT, LET in these sentences:

**a** He doesn't own the flat outright. He bought it on a 60-year _____.

**b** Since Mr Jones did not need to live in his cottage, he decided to _____ it to tourists.

**c** In order to show the training film to their salesmen, the New Art Manufacturing Company _____ a projector and screen for one day.

**d** Techno plc _____ an entire aircraft to fly 200 employees to Martinique for their annual holiday.

**e** As he was going to be in London for six months he decided to _____ a flat instead of staying in a hotel. He also decided to _____ a television rather than buy one.

**f** Silver Office Supplies does not buy vehicles directly. Its bank buys them and then _____ them to Silver Office Supplies.

**g** Mr and Mrs Gaskell _____ a cottage for their holiday in Devon.

**Exercise 11.7**
*Summary:*
*Making a list*

THE OFFICE MOVE: Exercises 11.7 – 11.12 are all about this topic.

For some time the directors of Abacus Ltd have been considering moving to a new office building. Recently, three reports arrived on the desk of Mr Thomas, the Managing Director. After reading these reports, Mr Thomas realised that a decision about the move had to be made quickly.

Read these extracts from the reports and make a list of the disadvantages of the present building.

In view of these disadvantages, what kind of building should Abacus move to? List the desirable features.

---

**1**

```
... our need to introduce new technology.  Although we have used
word processors for some years now, it is not possible to use them to
their full potential in this building, since there is not enough room for
each employee to have his or her own work-station.  We need at least
double our present floor area of 1500 square metres.  Furthermore, the
installation of modern data processing equipment, not to mention a digital
telephone exchange, is out of the question in the present building.
Ideally, we need a central computer to control all these systems, and also
to monitor heating and ventilation.  Sensors for fire and security could
also be linked to the computer.  To instal such a system requires many
kilometres of cables, and since the walls, floor and ceiling of the present
building are solid concrete, it is not practicable to cut the ducts for
laying cables.  Even at present, there are so many cables trailing across
the floor that staff are constantly tripping up.  If false floors and
ceilings are installed, the headroom in the office will be reduced to an
unacceptable level.

We must face the fact that the modern electronic systems we need to work
efficiently and profitably cannot ...
```

# UNIT ELEVEN

***Check your understanding 1*** **a**  Is this an internal report or does it come from outside the company?

   **b**  Complete the final sentence.

---

**2**

```
... settlement of the last insurance claim.  Although the warehouse
has a sprinkler system and heat and smoke sensors as a precaution
against fire, our inspector noted that the office building does not
have these things.  He also noted that the fire extinguishers were
often inaccessible, being hidden behind furniture and filing cabinets.
The absence of locks and grills on the ground floor windows is a
further cause for concern.  In view of these factors, it is likely
that the present premium will ...
```

---

***Check your understanding 2*** **c**  Who is this letter from?

   **d**  What do you think the writer is going to say next? Can you complete the last sentence?

---

**3**

```
... overcrowded offices and the general discomfort of working in the
building.  Every member of staff that I spoke to mentioned the breakdown
of the central heating system last winter.  The system is, by modern
standards, very inefficient, and does not heat the offices furthest away
from the boiler.  In addition, the lack of good ventilation, not to
mention air conditioning, makes the building stuffy in winter and humid
in summer.  The limited service in the staff canteen is another source
of bitter complaints.

Many people have complained that the car park is not large enough.
It seems that about a third of the staff who come by car have to park
outside in the road.  Furthermore, there is some resentment about reserved
parking spaces for managerial staff.

As trade union representative, I have been asked by my members to take up these
points with management with a view to ...
```

---

***Check your understanding 3*** **e**  Who wrote this?

   **f**  What does the writer want Mr Thomas to do immediately?

# UNIT ELEVEN

**Exercise 11.8**
*Discussion*

Read the details of office buildings that Abacus Ltd have received from estate agents.
Work in groups of three or four.
Discuss and decide which is the most suitable building for Abacus.
Use the list of desirable features that you have already made

```
NEW BRIDGE HOUSE

A newly-built, fully-fitted office building of 3,500 square metres on the
outskirts of Newbury.   Ready for immediate occupation

AMENITIES

*   service ducts for electronic cables
*   two eight-person passenger lifts
*   carpeted throughout
*   canteen facilities
*   car parking for 100 cars


TERMS

To let for a term of 25 years subject to five-yearly upward only rent reviews.
Alternatively, offers are invited for the freehold


RENT

£40,000 p.a.


RATES

£9,800 p.a.


VIEWING

Strictly by appointment with the sole agents:

DUFF & DUFF, 43 High Street, Newbury
Tel:  0635 56332
```

BARTON HOUSE

3,000 square metres. Located in the heart of Newbury, opposite the British Rail Station, this substantial office building has recently been renovated and refurbished to the highest standards.

AMENITIES

* adjacent to multi-storey car park
* gas central heating
* double glazing
* telephone and telex installed
* canteen facilities
* suspended ceiling

TERMS

To let for 25 years. Five-yearly rent reviews

RENT

£30,000 p.a.

RATES

£10,500 p.a.

VIEWING

Contact the Commercial Department of CHEETHAM & RUNNE, 10 River Lane, Newbury
Tel: 0635 99562

TALGARTH HOUSE

Excellent self-contained office suite of 2,800 square metres on the ground floor of this modern building. Centrally situated.

AMENITIES

● fully partitioned
● carpeted
● underground car park for 50 cars
● fluorescent lighting
● attractive reception area
● air conditioned
● central heating

TERMS

A new internal repairing and insuring lease to be agreed subject to rent reviews.

RENT

£20,000 pa

RATES

£6,000 pa

VIEWING

Strictly by appointment only through the sole agent:
FOX, BAXTER & SMITH, Tel: 0635 66111

*Check your understanding*   Which building –

    **a**   is not in the town centre?

    **b**   can be purchased instead of rented?

    **c**   does not have its own car park?

    **d**   is shared with other companies?

# UNIT ELEVEN

**Exercise 11.9**
*Listen to this*

The management of Abacus have decided to move their office to a new building. A working party consisting of senior management and a representative of the office workers has been set up to discuss the move.

The following agenda was circulated in the previous week.

```
OFFICE RELOCATION WORKING PARTY
_____

Thursday, 22nd January

10.00am - 11.00am

Managing Director's Office

A G E N D A

1       Reasons for the move

2       Organisation of the move

3       Implications of the move for office staff

4       A O B


cc      James Thomas
        Norman Smeaton
        Ray Simpson
        Bob Jones
```

Listen to the discussion at the meeting and answer these questions.

NORMAN SMEATON
DEPUTY MANAGING
DIRECTOR

RAY SIMPSON
CHIEF SALESMAN

BOB JONES
OFFICE WORKERS'
REPRESENTATIVE

What are the two letters that Norman Smeaton must write?

What must Ray Simpson do?

What are the six important pieces of information that Bob Jones must give to his members?

## UNIT ELEVEN

**Exercise 11.10**
*Reporting what people have said*

Study the following sentences, which are the exact words said by people at the meeting. Notice how the information can be reported to other people after the meeting.

What I'd really like to know, Mr Chairman, is how many jobs will survive automation?

Bob Jones asked how many jobs would survive automation.

If you study the plans of the new building carefully, you'll notice that there's an area provided for a showroom. All our new and best-selling lines will be on display there.

Norman Smeaton pointed out that if they studied the plans of the new building carefully, they would notice that there was an area provided for a showroom and added that all the new and best-selling lines would be on display there.

The technicians can't make the necessary ducts in the concrete floor.

Norman Smeaton explained that the technicians couldn't make the necessary ducts in the concrete floor.

Our present premises have proved unsuitable for the installation of electronic equipment.

Norman Smeaton said that the present premises had proved unsuitable for the installation of electronic equipment.

These examples follow the tense changes which are made in reported speech. However, we often report what people have said in words which express the same meaning, without necessarily following the tense change rules. For example:

Norman Smeaton pointed out that the plans of the new building contained a showroom area for the display of new and best-selling items.

How would you report Mr Thomas' suggestion?
'Let's move on to item two?'

## UNIT ELEVEN

Bob Jones is having lunch in the canteen when Mary Barton and Susan Brown come and sit with him. They want to know what happened at the meeting.

Use these extracts from what was said at the meeting to help you with Bob's answers.

NORMAN SMEATON:

> Office staff will be allowed an hour on the Friday to clear their desks, and will not be required to do any packing.

JAMES THOMAS:

> There are no plans for redundancies, but if the occasion arises we will certainly be prepared to consult the union.

BOB JONES:

> Some of my members are worried that they won't have enough time to do their shopping during the lunch hour.

NORMAN SMEATON:

> This problem can be solved by the introduction of the new flexi-time arrangements.

RAY SIMPSON:

> Will there be reserved car parking spaces for managerial staff?

JAMES THOMAS:

> No, there are no plans for reserved places. There will be plenty of room for everyone.

Use these words to introduce the information. They are not in order. Choose the word that goes best with the information you are reporting.

| | |
|---|---|
| stated | informed |
| promised | admitted |
| assured | claimed |
| explained | suggested |
| asked | refused |
| added | denied |
| replied | |

Working in groups of three, continue this dialogue. Remember that Susan and Mary want to know about the six things that affect them, which you have already listed in Exercise 11.9.

SUSAN BROWN:   What happened at the meeting, Bob? Anything to tell us?

BOB JONES:   Oh yes. Quite a lot. Mr Smeaton confirmed that the directors had decided to move to another building.

MARY BARTON:   Did he say when?

BOB JONES:   Yes, he said that the move would take place on Saturday 8th April.

SUSAN BROWN:   And will we . . .

## UNIT ELEVEN

**Exercise 11.11**
*Letter writing*

After the office relocation meeting Norman Smeaton made some notes on a sheet of paper with Abacus's present letterhead.

He asked you to write to the printers and order 5,000 sheets of paper with the new letterhead.

**a** Work with a partner and study the annotated letterhead. Write out the new letterhead.

**b** Make a plan for your order letter. Remember that Abacus regularly places orders with the printers.

**c** Write the required letter.

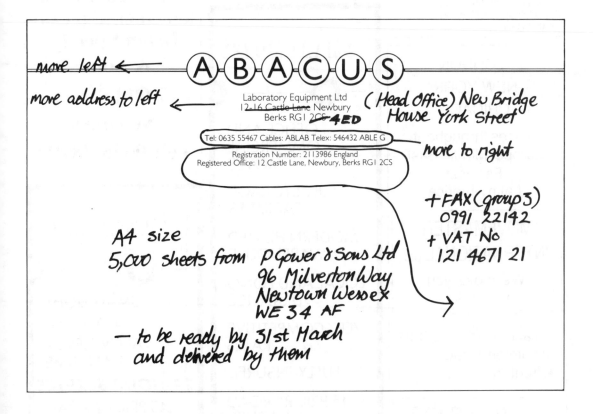

move left ←

move address to left ←

A B A C U S

Laboratory Equipment Ltd
12-16 Castle Lane Newbury
Berks RG1 2CS 4ED

(Head Office) New Bridge House York Street

Tel: 0635 55467 Cables: ABLAB Telex: 546432 ABLE G

move to right

Registration Number: 2113986 England
Registered Office: 12 Castle Lane, Newbury, Berks RG1 2CS

+ FAX (group 3)
0991 22142
+ VAT No
121 4671 21

A4 size
5,000 sheets from P Gower & Sons Ltd
96 Milverton Way
Newtown Wessex
WE 34 AF

— to be ready by 31st March
and delivered by them

# UNIT ELEVEN

**Exercise 11.12**
*Letter writing*

Norman Smeaton has asked you to look up removal firms in the local trade directory. He wants you to write to them, stating your requirements and asking for price quotations for the move.

**a** Work with a partner and study the page from the trade directory.
Choose the removal firm(s) you think most suitable.

**b** Make a plan for your letter. Check your plan with the list of functions in Unit Two, selecting appropriate structures.

**c** Write the required letter.

---

REMOVALS AND STORAGE
(cont'd)

Mercury Light Removals Ltd
52 Oakley Avenue Newbury
Tel: 0635 9417

LONDON
NEW YORK
CHICAGO

Offices throughout
Europe, Middle East
Far East,
Latin America

**MOVEMASTER
INTERNATIONAL** plc

We move you
worldwide

Upland Trading Estate
Middleton Road
Alfredton

Tel: **3232 6492**

Quick Flit Domestic Moves Ltd
12 Grange Road    Newbury
Tel: 0635 4456

Rogers Removals
'One Man and his van'
Newbury 0635 4632

OFFICE AND
COMMERCIAL
MOVES

FULL STORAGE
FACILITIES

MODERN HEATED
WAREHOUSE

LOCAL AND LONG
DISTANCE

VERY COMPETITIVE
RATES

FULLY-INSURED

45 PRIORY ROAD
NEWBURY

**TEL:
0635 6792**

**Household Removal
Established 150 years**
**RELIABLE AND FAST**
**Brian Speedy
& Sons**

**17 Old Street
Newbury**
**Tel: 0635 78994**

SMALL LIGHT
REMOVALS

ANYWHERE –
ANYTIME
*24-HOUR SERVICE*
45 PRIORY ROAD
NEWBURY

**TEL:
0635 5564**

**Exercise 11.13**
*Listen to this:*
*Making a hotel reservation*

Read the letter Caroline Hobbs has written to confirm Mr Patterson's hotel reservation in Edinburgh.

Listen to her telephone conversation with the receptionist at the Barnes Hotel, London (see advertisement).

Note the information you need to:

**a** Write a letter to Barnes Hotel confirming the reservation
**b** Write a memo to Mr Patterson telling him what he needs to know.

Will the letter and the memo contain the same information?

---

# THE OLD COUNTRY CLOTHING COMPANY

1195–1200 North Lakeside Drive
Montreal P.Q. H3B 1X9
CANADA
Tel: 538 6408
Telex: 189123 COUNTCL C
Cables: COUNTRYCLOTH

The Manager
The Arden House Hotel
1 Charlotte Street
Edinburgh
E1A 2AA
Scotland

19 February 19-

Dear Sir,

Further to our telephone conversation this morning, I am writing to confirm that you have agreed to reserve a single room for Mr William Patterson for the night of 11 March.

Yours faithfully,

*Catherine Hobbs*

Catherine Hobbs
PA to Mr William Patterson

---

## ══════ B A R N E S   H O T E L ══════

1 Hyde Avenue (overlooking Hyde Park)
London SW1 4BB

Tariff: double (twin beds) £150 per night
single £100 per night

- 400 rooms
- Gresham restaurant (chef: Antony Moss)
- Grill Room
- Seafood Bar
- Henry's Cocktail Lounge
- roof garden

- presidential suite
- underground car park
- fitness centre (with jacuzzi and Nautilus equipment)
- business communication centre
- all major credit cards accepted

──── RESERVATIONS: 01 555 0043 ────

# UNIT ELEVEN

## The London Stock Exchange

At the end of the sixteenth century the first joint-stock companies were formed in England to trade overseas, eg, the East India Company (1600) which traded in India. In order to establish these companies, a number of people contributed sums of money and then shared the profit or accepted the loss when the company began trading. Each person's contribution was divided into shares – £1,000 would be divided into 1,000 £1 shares, for example. If the company did well, the shareholders could sell all or some of their shares at a higher price than they had paid for them to people who wanted to have a share of the company's profit, or who expected that the price of a share would increase even more and that they could sell at a profit too. A market in shares developed in the coffee houses of the City of London. At first it was an unregulated market and in 1720 many people lost their money in the 'South Sea Bubble' when the South Sea Company collapsed.

In 1801 the Stock Exchange was formed and soon became the accepted place to buy and sell shares. One reason for its success was the fact that people would be compensated if a member of the Stock Exchange behaved dishonestly. The Stock Exchange was formed as a private organisation whose members could be expelled if they did not maintain the highest standards.

The way of doing business on the Stock Exchange changed over the years but by the end of the nineteenth century members were divided into two groups – stockbrokers, who bought and sold shares for their clients and charged fixed rates of commission for this service, and stockjobbers who bought and sold shares on their own account. Brokers bought shares from jobbers, who made money from the difference between their selling price and their buying price. Jobbers had 'pitches', rather like market stalls, on the trading floor of the Stock Exchange where brokers would go to buy or sell according to their clients' instructions. Jobbers were not allowed to sell directly to the public, and brokers were not allowed to sell their own shares to their clients.

During the 1970s it became clear that this system would not allow London to compete successfully as an international financial market place with the larger stock markets in New York and Tokyo. In particular, the firms of jobbers and brokers were very small in comparison with the American and Japanese investment banks. Consequently, on 27th October 1986, on a day known as 'Big Bang', the system described above was abolished.

There were four main changes. Firstly, there is no longer any distinction between broker and jobber. All member firms of the Stock Exchange can now buy from and sell to their clients. Secondly, fixed commissions were abolished. This makes little difference to the individual but it means that large purchasers of shares, such as insurance companies can negotiate very low charges. Thirdly, firms outside the Stock Exchange, such as British and foreign banks were allowed to become members of the Stock Exchange, and fourthly, a new computerised dealing system – Stock Exchange Automated Quotations – was introduced.

The effect of these changes was that many firms of jobbers and brokers became part of large financial groups centred on banks. These became 'market makers'. This means that they committed themselves to always offering a buying and a selling price in a range of shares. There are also 'broker dealers' who buy from and sell to their clients, but do not always 'make a market', and 'agency brokers' who, as before, act only as agents for investors and charge commission. Because of the new computerised dealing system the trading floor of the Stock Exchange is much less busy, since dealers buy and sell 'off-screen' in their offices, instead of face to face on the trading floor. Many firms have moved into new offices with huge dealing rooms full of the latest electronic equipment with which they can deal in Tokyo and New York as well as in London.

Because of the pace of technological change and the intensity of competition, it is likely that the number of firms dealing in shares will become fewer and larger.

The prices of shares change from day to day according to supply and demand and the rise or fall of the market is measured by the Financial Times' 30-share Index which records movements in the share prices of thirty large companies. People who believe that prices will rise are called 'bulls', and those who believe that prices will fall are known as 'bears'. People who buy new issues of shares and sell immediately in the hope of making a profit are called 'stags'. Large profits were made by 'stags' in 1984–7 when the government sold (or 'privatised') nationalised industries such as British Telecom, British Gas and British Airways. From 1973 to 1987 share prices rose steadily, although there were falls from time to time. It was a 'bull market'. However, in the week beginning 19 October 1987 there were sudden and dramatic falls in share prices on all the world stock markets. Some people expected prices to rise again, but others believed that this was the beginning of a long-term 'bear market' and a worldwide economic recession. They compared it to the Great Crash of 1929 and the recession of the 1930s.

## DRAPERY AND STORES—Cont.

| 1987 High | Low | Stock | Price | + or − | Div Net | C'vr | Y'ld Gr's | P/E |
|---|---|---|---|---|---|---|---|---|
| 193 | 130 | Tip Top 10p | 165xd | +2 | 2.0 | 1.0 | 1.7 | 80.4 |
| *135 | 70 | Top Value Inds 10p | 120xr | +5 | 2.5 | 3.4 | 2.9 | 13.1 |
| 264 | 171½ | Underwoods 10p | 204 | | 2.5 | 2.5 | 1.7 | 32.6 |
| *133 | 111½ | Upton (E.) | 120xa | +5 | — | — | — | — |
| 216 | 95 | Usher (Frank) 5p | 211 | +1 | 5.5 | 2.6 | 3.6 | 14.9 |
| *302 | 114 | Vivat Hldgs | 263 | −2 | gh2.5 | 4.4 | 1.3 | 21.3 |
| 437 | 278 | Ward White | 409 | | ↑7.5 | 3.0 | 2.5 | 17.3 |
| 161½ | 107 | Do Cnv Red Prf 10p | 144 | | 6.0 | — | 5.7 | — |
| 275 | 73 | Wassall (J. W.) | 180 | | 1.0 | 1.9 | 0.8 | — |
| 355 | 255 | Wickes | 347xd | +2 | 2.5 | 5.1 | 1.0 | 27.3 |
| 127 | 115 | Do. 5½pc Sub.Cv.Ln.' | 127 | | Q5.5% | — | f4.4 | — |
| 315 | 153 | Wigfalls | 268 | −1 | 2.5 | 0.3 | 1.3 | — |
| 260 | 148 | Wilding Off. Eqp. 10p | 253 | | u3.25 | 2.3 | 1.8 | 33.4 |
| 142 | 68 | Windsmoor 5p | 132 | | 2.0 | 4.3 | 2.1 | 15.4 |
| 215 | 80 | Wooltons B'ware10p | 190 | −2 | dR3.7 | 1.5 | 2.7 | 34.1 |
| 461 | 329 | Woolworth Hldgs | 358 | +5 | ↑8.0 | 2.5 | 3.1 | 15.8 |
| £206 | £150 | Do. 8½pc Ln 2000 | £161 | | 8½% | — | f5.4 | — |
| 153 | 122 | World of Leather 10p | 135 | +2 | d3.0 | 3.3 | 3.0 | 13.4 |

*(leftmost detached P/E column: P/E, (42.5), 19.6, 11.8, φ, 12.4, 12.6, 16.8, —, 11.4, 19.2, 14.3, 22.3, 19.0, 17.3, 20.3, 20.9, 21.3, 15.2, 13.2, 20.2, 15.0, 9.1, 8.8, 9.9, 4.3)*

## ELECTRICALS

| High | Low | Stock | Price | + or − | Div Net | C'vr | Y'ld Gr's | P/E |
|---|---|---|---|---|---|---|---|---|
| 455 | 332 | AB Electronic | 455 | +41 | G12.5 | φ | 3.9 | φ |
| 83 | 46 | AMS Inds 5p | 59 | +1 | 1.5 | 3.3 | 3.5 | 11.8 |
| 74 | 43 | Acorn Cmptr 10p | 55 | +1 | — | — | — | φ |
| 180 | 143 | Admiral Computing 5p | 145 | +2 | u2.13 | 3.6 | 2.1 | 19.0 |
| 470 | 207 | Alphameric 5p | 424 | −1 | 2.5 | 6.4 | 0.8 | 26.6 |
| 46½ | 27½ | Amer Elect Comp 5p | 38 | −1 | ↑0.87 | 2.7 | 3.2 | 12.8 |
| 325 | 129 | | | | | | | |

## DRAPERY AND STORES—Contd

| 1988 High | Low | Stock | Price | + or − | Div Net | C'vr | Y'ld Gr's | P/E |
|---|---|---|---|---|---|---|---|---|
| 80 | 58 | Upton (E.) y | 70 | | — | — | — | — |
| 160 | 140 | Usher (Frank) 5p.. y | 140 | | Ka6.0 | 2.6 | 5.7 | 9.9 |
| 181 | 130 | Vivat Hldgs y | 138 | +7 | tgh2.5 | 4.4 | 2.4 | 11.2 |
| 341 | 294 | Ward White a | 310 | −3 | 8.75 | φ | 3.8 | φ |
| 129 | 111 | Do Cnv Red Prf 10p. y | 113 | | 6.0 | — | 7.1 | — |
| 125 | 100 | Wassall (J. W.) | 110 | | 1.0 | 1.9 | 1.2 | — |
| *270 | 232 | Wickes y | 260 | +1 | ga1.5 | 10.9 | 0.8 | 16.6 |
| 226 | 155 | Wigfalls y | 223 | | ↑2.5 | 0.3 | 1.5 | — |
| 215 | 160 | Wilding Off. 10p.. y | 207 | +5 | 3.25 | 3.5 | 2.1 | 18.2 |
| 127 | 80 | Windsmoor 5p a | 125 | | ↑3.25 | φ | 3.5 | φ |
| 170 | 98 | Wooltons B'ware10p. y | 145 | −5 | dR3.7 | 2.3 | 3.4 | 17.2 |
| 307 | 249 | Woolworth Hldgs.. a | 283 | +9 | 9.0 | φ | 4.3 | φ |
| £143 | £121 | Do. 8½pc Ln 2000.. y | £130 | | 8½% | — | 6.5 | — |
| 155 | 90 | World of Leather 10p. y | 100 | +2 | 3.2 | 2.1 | 4.3 | 13.9 |

## ELECTRICALS

| High | Low | Stock | Price | + or − | Div Net | C'vr | Y'ld Gr's | P/E |
|---|---|---|---|---|---|---|---|---|
| 445 | 340 | AB Electronic β | 406 | +1 | †12.5 | 1.9 | 4.1 | 16.4 |
| 54 | 31 | AMS Inds 5p y | 46 | −2 | 1.5 | 2.5 | 4.3 | 12.2 |
| 37 | 23 | Acorn Cmptr 10p. y | 25 | | — | — | — | — |
| 120 | 87 | Admiral Computing 5p. y | 116xd | | 1.46 | 5.3 | 1.7 | 14.5 |
| 116 | 88 | Alba 10p y | 100 | | K4.35 | 2.2 | 5.8 | 10.2 |
| *283 | 209 | Alphameric 5p y | 283xr | | K3.5 | 6.4 | 1.6 | 18.3 |
| 178 | 113 | Amstrad 5p a | 174 | +4 | ↑0.7 | 25.5 | 0.5 | 9.0 |
| 362 | 262 | Appl d H'graphics 5p.. β | 280 | | — | — | — | — |
| 335 | 240 | Do Warrants y | 240 | | — | — | — | — |
| 114 | 94 | Apricot Comp 10p. a | 101 | | 2.0 | φ | 2.7 | φ |
| 68 | 40 | Arcolectric 'A' NV 5p y | 63 | +1 | 0.88 | φ | 1.9 | φ |
| 170 | 110 | | | | | | 3.0 | 11.7 |

**Exercise 11.14**
*Things to find out* Find out about one of these topics and report what you have learnt in writing or as a short talk.

**a** new technology in financial markets
**b** a stock market in your country
**c** successful investment

# *U N I T   T W E L V E* *Revision and consolidation*

**Exercise 12.1**
*Letter writing*

Compare the points made by Mr Smeaton and Mr Smart in these two letters. A further letter is clearly required. Write it, for Mr Smeaton's signature.

Laboratory Equipment Ltd (Head Office)
New Bridge House York Street
Newbury Berks RG1 4ED

Tel: 0991 55467 Cables: ABLAB Telex: 546432 ABLE G
Fax (group 3): 0635 22142 VAT No: 121 4671 21

Registration No: 2113986 England
Registered Office: New Bridge House, York Street, Newbury
Berks RG1 4ED

Mr J Smart
Smart Moves Ltd
45 Priory Road
Newbury
Berks
RG3 4AH

13 April 19-

Dear Mr Smart

I am writing concerning the removal of our office furniture and equipment from our old premises in Castle Lane to our new premises at the above address on 7 April.

Unfortunately, I have to inform you that we are not entirely satisfied with the service which we received. Firstly, although it was agreed that work would start at 9am, your vans did not arrive until 10.05 am, and your foreman gave no explanation for the delay. As a result of the late start, there was not enough time for your removal men to unpack all the items at the end of the day. Consequently, on Monday morning, our own staff had to finish the job. This not only delayed the start of our work but also led to a dispute with the union representative.

Secondly, although you had assured us that you would send four large vans, only three arrived. The strenuous efforts of your men to load everything into these three vans resulted in damage to a photocopier, which has cost us £350 to repair.

Thirdly, we cannot understand why your vans took an hour and five minutes to travel from Castle Lane to New Bridge House - a distance of three miles!

Finally, we were very surprised on Monday morning to discover that your men had delivered six filing cabinets and a table which do not belong to us.

We expected a higher standard of service from your company, which has enjoyed a good reputation locally.

We would appreciate an explanation of these matters and must insist that you compensate us for the cost of repairs to our photocopier and collect the wrongly-delivered items.

We look forward to your reply.

Yours sincerely

Norman Smeaton
Deputy Managing Director

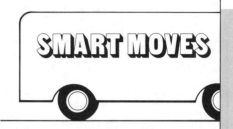

Smart Moves Ltd
45 Priory Road
Newbury
Berks RG3 4AH

Tel: 0635 6792
Cables: SMARTMOVE
Fax: (group 3) 0635 8846

Mr Norman Smeaton
Deputy Managing Director
Abacus Laboratory Equipment Ltd
Head Office
New Bridge House
York Street
Newbury
Berks
RG1 4ED                                          17 April 19-

Dear Mr Smeaton

Thank you for your letter of 13 April in which you informed us of the
problems you experienced during your recent office move.  We are always
interested in receiving comments from our customers because this helps us
to improve our service.

I have investigated the matters you refer to, and I accept that you have
good reason to complain as, on this occasion, we do not seem to have
reached our usual high standards.

However, this was largely due to circumstances beyond our control.  We did
send four vans, but one was involved in an accident, which also delayed
the other three.  I am surprised our foreman did not explain this to you.
The journey from Castle Lane to New Bridge House took longer than usual
because of roadworks at the Kingfisher roundabout.

We offer our sincere apologies and have reduced your bill by £150 in
compensation for the inconvenience you have suffered.

Yours sincerely

*John Smart*

John Smart
Manager

**Exercise 12.2**  Read David Jackson's memo and write an appropriate letter
*Letter writing*  for him to sign.

—————————— Memo ——————————

To : Paula Armstrong      Date: 5th April
                          Reference:

From : David Jackson

Subject : Letter from Perfect Plastics about non-payment

Please reply to this letter from Perfect Plastics. They
complain that we haven't paid for order no 55412,
but I've checked our bank statement and
the payment has gone through (see attached copy—
its cheque no. 1961). Give them all the details
If the money has left our account, it should
be in theirs. They've obviously got themselves in
a muddle over this (better not say that—'may
have overlooked receipt of payment' is the way
to put it, I think). I notice that Perfect Plastics
changed their bank recently. Tell them to check
with both banks—'advise you to make enquiries
of your current and former bankers', that's the
phrase to use. Tell them to get in touch again
if they can't sort it out at their end.

```
┌─────────────────────────────────────────────────────────────────┐
│  FINLAYS BANK PLC                                                 │
│                                                                   │
│  ACCOUNT No   98 564 32768                                   O     │
│                                                                   │
│  SILVER OFFICE SUPPLIES LTD                                       │
│                                                             O     │
│  STATEMENT OF ACCOUNT No  361                                     │
├──────────┬──────────┬───────────┬──────────┬─────────────────────┤
│ DATE     │ NUMBER   │ DEBIT     │ CREDIT   │ BALANCE             │
├──────────┼──────────┼───────────┼──────────┼─────────────────────┤
│ 29 MARCH │   1954   │ C £5,500  │  NIL     │ £113,280            │
│ 29 MARCH │   1957   │ C £  800  │          │ £112,480            │
│ 30 MARCH │   1959   │ C £2,130  │          │ £110,350            │
│ 30 MARCH │   1961   │ C £1,870  │          │ £108,480            │
│          │          │           │          │                     │
├──────────┴──────────┴───────────┴──────────┴─────────────────────┤
│  D  Deposit          T  Transfer          C  Cheque              │
│  S  Standing Order   DD Direct Debit      OD Overdrawn           │
├──────────────────────────────┬────────────────────────────────────┤
│ TOTAL CREDITS        NIL      │ TOTAL DEBITS      £10,300   O      │
│ PREVIOUS BALANCE              │ CURRENT BALANCE                    │
│   27 MARCH   £118,780         │   1 APRIL   £108,480        O      │
└──────────────────────────────┴────────────────────────────────────┘
```

**Exercise 12.3**
*Vocabulary*

Read this list of words. Work with a partner. Make SEVEN groups of FOUR related words.

For example: refund
                  expenses
                  discount
                  quotation
These are all to do with money.

| | | |
|---|---|---|
| message | ferry | load |
| vessel | memo | factory |
| representative | consignment | cargo |
| plant | report | consultant |
| discount | invoice | bonus |
| commission | document | certificate |
| premises | expenses | broker |
| fee | salary | refund |
| van | statement | note |
| warehouse | lorry | shipment |
| quotation | agent | |

**Exercise 12.4**
*Oral summary*

a  Find the sentence which best summarises this article.
b  Give an oral summary of the article. Identify the cause of the problem, the effects and possible solution.

# Slow payers owe £57 billion and curb job creation

Small firms are owed a total of £57 billion by slow payers, which is restricting their ability to create new jobs, according to the Forum of Private Business.

The Forum's Chief Executive, Stan Mendham, said that the main culprits were large companies, who were responsible for seven out of ten of all slow paid invoices.

Speaking at a press conference at the House of Commons as part of a campaign for legislation which would enable firms to charge interest on late paid bills, he said that the average time lag for invoices being paid was seventy-five days.

This resulted in business failure and lack of growth. The restriction of cash flow resulted in increased borrowing and reduced profits, which in turn damaged the ability of small firms to create jobs.

Mr Mendham said that all other EEC countries, except Ireland, had a law entitling creditors to interest for late payment of debts.

One Forum member, Peter Rolf, managing director of Yarmouth Steels, said that his company was currently owed £700,000, mostly by large firms. 'If one third of that was paid we'd save something like £25,000 in bank charges. We could use that money to employ two extra people.'

The only government action so far has been to introduce a voluntary code of conduct on payment, which small firms believe is inadequate and ineffective.

**Exercise 12.5**
*Letter writing*

Angus MacDonald is working in his office when his telex machine prints out this message:

```
132876 WHIGH G

876945 COUNTCL C

ATTN MACDONALD

RE TWEED CONSIGNMENT ORDER 5512

TWENTY ROLLS GREY BLACK HERRINGBONE MISSING WHEN SHIP UNLOADED SUSPECT
THEFT REMAINDER OF ORDER OK REQUIRE REPLACEMENTS URGENTLY CAN YOU SUPPLY?
LETTER FOLLOWS

PATTERSON
876945 COUNTCL C

132876 WHIGH G
```

a  Write a letter, for Bill Patterson to sign, to follow the telex.
b  Write a letter, for Angus MacDonald to sign, to Amalgamated Insurance.

# WORDLISTS

**Commercial vocabulary** These are the commercial words used in this book. The number after the word refers to the unit in which it first appears.

| | | | | | |
|---|---|---|---|---|---|
| accepting house | 6 | co-operative | 4 | government securities | 5 |
| accident report form | 10 | cost & freight | 2 | graph | 10 |
| accounts | 1 | cost, insurance, freight | 2 | gross | 7 |
| advertisement | 1 | courtesy car | 2 | guarantee | 4 |
| agency broker | 11 | covering letter | 1 | | |
| agenda | 11 | current account | 6 | handling | 7 |
| agent | 7 | curriculum vitae | 1 | hire | 11 |
| analysis | 7 | customs clearance | 7 | homeworker | 10 |
| application form | 1 | | | | |
| assets | 9 | dead-end job | 4 | import | 2 |
| authorise | 9 | deadline | 5 | inspector | 7 |
| | | dealing room | 10 | insurance | 3 |
| balance of payments | 5 | debts | 9 | interest rate | 10 |
| balance of trade | 5 | deduction | 9 | in transit | 7 |
| bar chart | 10 | deficit | 5 | irrevocable | 5 |
| bear | 11 | delivered duty paid | 3 | insurance | 3 |
| bill | 3 | delivery | 3 | invisible trade | 5 |
| bill of exchange | 3 | demonstration | 3 | issuing bank | 5 |
| bill of lading | 5 | deposit | 12 | item | 9 |
| bonus | 1 | deposit account | 6 | | |
| book-keeping | 1 | design fault | 9 | joint stock | 11 |
| booklet | 5 | despatch | 4 | | |
| branch | 6 | direct debit | 12 | launch | 2 |
| breakage | 7 | discontinue | 11 | leaflet | 5 |
| break-in | 9 | discount | 2 | lease | 11 |
| brochure | 2 | dispute | 11 | legal proceedings | 10 |
| broker dealers | 11 | diversify | 7 | let | 11 |
| brokers | 1 | documentary credits | 3 | liaison | 1 |
| building society | 1 | documents against acceptance | 3 | limited liability | 4 |
| bulk carrier | 7 | documents against payment | 3 | line | 3 |
| bulk order | 5 | | | luncheon voucher | 1 |
| bull | 11 | enclosure | 1 | | |
| business card | 4 | estimate | 3 | market share | 2 |
| | | eurodollars | 6 | mass-produced | 10 |
| career | 1 | expenses | 9 | media | 2 |
| cargo | 3 | export | 3 | merchandise | 9 |
| cash flow | 12 | ex-works | 3 | merchant banking | 6 |
| catalogue | 2 | | | microcomputer | 1 |
| charter | 7 | face value | 5 | model | 3 |
| circa | 1 | facsimile | 9 | | |
| claim | 7 | flexi-time | 11 | nationalised industry | 4 |
| classified advertising | 1 | foreman | 12 | negotiable | 1 |
| clearing bank | 6 | forward price | 10 | net | 10 |
| clearing house | 6 | franchise | 8 | network | 8 |
| clients | 11 | franco | 3 | notify | 7 |
| commercial invoice | 3 | freehold | 11 | | |
| commission | 1 | free alongside ship | 3 | open account trading | 3 |
| commodity | 7 | free on board | 3 | open outcry | 10 |
| commute | 10 | free on board airport | 3 | output | 10 |
| compensation | 9 | free on rail | 3 | overdrawn | 12 |
| confirming bank | 5 | freight | 3 | overheads | 10 |
| consequential loss | 7 | fringe benefits | 1 | | |
| consignee | 10 | gilts | 5 | pamphlet | 2 |
| consignment | 7 | giro transfer | 8 | parcel | 7 |
| consultant | 1 | good prospects | 1 | partners | 1 |
| container traffic | 7 | goods | 3 | partnership | 4 |

| | | | | | |
|---|---|---|---|---|---|
| penalty clause | 7 | research and development | 10 | surplus | 5 |
| personnel manager | 1 | retail | 1 | syndicate | 9 |
| pie chart | 2 | return | 9 | | |
| plant | 9 | risk | 3 | table of statistics | 10 |
| policy | 9 | royalty | 8 | tangible goods | 5 |
| post code | 1 | rush hour | 11 | target audience | 2 |
| premises | 9 | | | telex | 7 |
| premium | 9 | salary | 1 | terms of payment | 2 |
| price list | 2 | sample | 1 | time lag | 12 |
| price quotation | 3 | satellite dish | 7 | toll free | 2 |
| priority | 11 | scheduled flights | 7 | tramp ship | 7 |
| private limited company | 4 | season ticket | 1 | treasury bills | 5 |
| productivity | 1 | settlement | 10 | turnover | 10 |
| pro-forma invoice | 3 | shipment | 5 | | |
| promotion | 1 | showroom | 11 | under separate cover | 3 |
| proposal form | 9 | signatory | 10 | underwriter | 9 |
| public limited company | 4 | sole proprietor | 4 | | |
| purchase | 2 | sole trader | 4 | visible trade | 5 |
| | | specifications | 7 | | |
| range | 2 | speculator | 10 | warehouse | 3 |
| receipt | 2 | spot price | 10 | witness | 9 |
| recipient | 1 | staff | 1 | word processor | 1 |
| recruit | 4 | stag | 11 | workforce | 10 |
| redundancy | 11 | stock | 3 | working party | 11 |
| referee | 1 | stocklist | 11 | workplace | 10 |
| renew | 9 | submit | 9 | workspace | 10 |
| representative | 3 | supplement | 9 | workstation | 11 |

## Office technology

| | | | | | |
|---|---|---|---|---|---|
| answer back code | 7 | ducts | 11 | satellite dish | 7 |
| antennae | 11 | facsimile | 10 | scanner | 7 |
| central heating | 11 | fluorescent lighting | 11 | screen | 3 |
| compatible | 10 | grills | 11 | sensors | 11 |
| data processing | 11 | keyboard | 3 | sprinkler system | 11 |
| digital pulse | 10 | microcomputer | 1 | telex | 7 |
| digital technology | 10 | monitor | 3 | word processor | 1 |
| disc | 3 | printer | 3 | | |
| double glazing | 11 | print out | 7 | | |

## Useful phrases

**(coll = colloquial)**

| | | | | | |
|---|---|---|---|---|---|
| act as a referee | 1 | follow instructions | 8 | pay attention to detail | 1 |
| arrange a meeting | 2 | found a company | 8 | pick up the stuff (coll) | 10 |
| assess risk | 9 | fulfil an order | 9 | place an order | 10 |
| associate with | 9 | gain experience | 1 | place the matter in the | |
| be entitled to | 10 | get blood out of a stone (coll) | 11 | hands of a solicitor | 10 |
| cater for | 1 | get in touch (coll) | 12 | play a major part in | 3 |
| cause for concern | 11 | get rid of (coll) | 9 | present documents | 5 |
| certify that | 10 | give some advice | 4 | put it bluntly (coll) | 9 |
| chase something up (coll) | 10 | give someone a bad name (coll) | 9 | quote a discount | 2 |
| clear an account | 10 | have a word with someone (coll) | 5 | seek advice | 9 |
| climb steeply | 10 | honour a contract | 9 | sell like hot cakes (coll) | 9 |
| complete a checklist | 1 | in accordance with | 10 | set a deadline for | 10 |
| consist of | 11 | in excess of | 9 | settle an account | 10 |
| cope with | 1 | lay out a letter | 1 | sort something out (coll) | 12 |
| decline steadily | 10 | liaise with | 1 | stand for | 3 |
| desirable features | 11 | make a mess of (coll) | 10 | start from scratch (coll) | 9 |
| dispose of | 9 | marked improvement | 9 | stay put (coll) | 9 |
| do business with | 5 | meet a deadline | 5 | submit a claim for expenses | 9 |
| draft a letter | 5 | meet our requirements | 5 | take steps to secure payment | 10 |
| fall to a low of | 10 | obtain a discount | 3 | work under pressure | 1 |